If
Mama
Ain't
Happy

Celine Sparks

Publishing Designs, Inc.
Huntsville, Alabama

Publishing Designs, Inc.
P.O. Box 3241
Huntsville, Alabama 35810

Unless noted, scriptures are from ESV® Bible

Front cover art: Phyllis Alexander

Cover and text design: Crosslin Creative

Editors: Peggy Coulter and Debra G. Wright

Printed in the United States of America

Publisher's Cataloging-in-Publication Data

Sparks, Celine, 1965—
If Mama Ain't Happy / Celine Sparks.
204 pages
Thirteen chapters.
1. Attitude. 2. Biblical motivation. 3. Humor.
I. Title.
ISBN 978-1-945127-24-3
248.8

Dedication

*To Mattianne, whose deep
compassion crowded out her stubborn will*

Endorsements

Reading this book is like chatting with an encouraging (and witty!) friend. Every chapter brings us to a crossroads, where Celine offers two opposing reactions to everyday situations. Celine's humor will immediately draw you in, and her warmth and godly wisdom will leave you inspired to step forward in faith. I adore her creative approach to "speaking the truth in love"!

—**Kristin Hicks**, author at The Ruffled Mango online

Celine Sparks has written books and articles, participated on many lectureship programs, and spoken at a number of ladies' days. Her latest book is *If Mama Ain't Happy*. Although designed for ladies, I had the privilege of reading this very fine work. As the title suggests, it is about happiness. You will find it difficult to put this book down after you start reading it. With her great sense of humor, she has produced a volume that is witty, laugh-out-loud funny, and yet, thought-provoking. Her true-to-life illustrations and lessons will greatly benefit all readers.

—**David Lipe**, PhD, retired Bible professor FHU,
author of Commentary on John and other books

If Mama Ain't Happy gives us practical examples of what barriers to biblical happiness may look like in our lives, and it uses humor, personal experience, and knowledge gained from studying God's Word to challenge us to recognize and overcome those barriers. Celine Sparks touches our heartstrings and our funny bones with her teachable-moment stories about potlucks, family photo sessions, grandparents' love, fireworks, and even biscuits in a way like no other to encourage us to live as God intended. Her insights coupled with her guided Bible study are beneficial to women of all ages and all circumstances as we seek and share the joy that can be found in Christ Jesus.

—**Debbie McLaughlin**, Executive Coordinator -
FHU Associates

You know a book is good when you can't wait to tell others all about it. Conviction plus humor is a powerful combination, and *If Mama Ain't Happy* has plenty of both. It's real. It's relatable. And you can't help but come away from this study with a better heart posture.

—**Kathy Pollard**, author of Return to Me

Contents

Introduction

It's been a tough year. Disease has been rampant, the grave has robbed us of some of our youngest and brightest, the physical storms have been ferocious, and divorce has destroyed some of the homes closest to us. I didn't realize I had this many tears.

Yeah, I did just start the first words of this book with a downer, but don't lay it down yet. There's not a tear big enough to drown out the love of God, the comfort of his presence, the understanding that he is working it all for our benefit.

If Mama ain't happy, has she considered the impact of that kind of a relationship? I've heard preachers say that God never promised us happiness. Maybe so. But he told us how to get it, how to maintain it, and how to hold on to it tight when the enemy tries to rob us of it.

The world doesn't have that. Oh they grab at happiness by the big handfuls just to open up empty calloused hands before giving it another try. Real happiness doesn't work that way. Thank God it doesn't work that way!

It resides in the heart and not in the hands. It thrives on trust, it's fortified in trials, and it puts down its roots in resignation of self. It's like the two-year-old on the top of the slide. It's not coming down.

This book explores the decisions we make to arrive at the place we want to be, but at best it's a hem-book. It touches the hem of the garment, and hopefully drives us to examine scripture a little closer, to live life a little better; to get past just the hem.

It's a book about happiness. Oh, you can insist on only calling it joy if you want to play the game of semantics, but I'd rather play the game of Hungry Hungry Hippos. It ends faster and someone wins.

After all, scripture itself says "Happy is the man who finds wisdom, and the man who gains understanding" (Prov. 3:13 NKJV). Let's turn the page and try to do both.

1

IF MAMA AIN'T HAPPY,

Is She Worried?

Worrying or Casting

Moms worry. We worry about whether or not the seventh grader remembered to put on deodorant before marching with the band on a 103-degree afternoon. We worry that the ninth grader forgot to feed the cat. By the time that eleventh grader rolls around, we can't enjoy the fact that he's out at a nice restaurant for worrying he'll forget to leave a tip on the table. Or what if he leaves too little? Or too much?

Those are the crazy worries. It's not that we worry about something that's not going to happen. But if we're not careful, we'll worry about something that definitely is going to happen and probably already has. Kids are going to handle things like kids handle them, and no worry up front, during, or afterward can change that. I came up with this worry list a while back of some ridiculous things that might seem paramount to some of us at the time.

○ When company comes, will a mouse run across the room?

○ When I'm vacuuming, will I vacuum up the diamond that fell out of my ring last year?

○ When I'm cleaning, will I accidentally mix bleach and ammonia and everyone will die?

○ Will I get invited to someone important's house like a state senator or Eli Gold, and then spill my drink all over the fancy tablecloth?

○ Or will something fall out of my nose when the hors d'oeuvres are being passed, and it will become one of them?

○ And what happens to people when they are voted off the island on a reality TV show? Are they just drifting at sea now?

○ Will someone forget to bring two #2 pencils to the ACT test?

○ Was I paying attention to the flight attendant when she explained how to remove the seat cushion to make it a floatation device?

○ When I'm walking to my car in the parking lot, will I drop my bag that looks like a grocery bag, and everyone will know that I really bought were tampons and Preparation H?

○ What if my slip falls to my ankles when I am walking down the hall of a grand hotel during the busiest convention of the year?

○ What if I drink a forty-four-ounce drink on a road trip and then pass a sign that says "Next exit, forty-nine miles"?

○ Was my mother right that when I wear underwear with holes in them and I get blown away in a tornado, I will be really embarrassed when they find me?

Do we worry like that?

Sweating the Small Stuff

There are what we call big worries, and there are little worries. My favorite poet, Shel Silverstein, has a children's poem called *Whatif*, and just after the worries,

"Whatif the fish won't bite?" and "Whatif the wind tears up my kite?" come these two: "Whatif they start a war? Whatif my parents get divorced?" Quite a range. There's quite a range between a sandcastle and a seashore, but they're made up of the same thing.

I once worried that my son who was visiting his cousin on a college campus would go through all his clothes the first day and not have a thing to wear the other days. Or else he would just keep wearing the first thing he had on the entire week and forget about his other clothes altogether. I talked to him about it, but I did more than that. I'm kind of embarrassed to say that I got some masking tape, and labeled each shirt on the inside neck-hole—Thursday, Friday, Saturday, Sunday, Monday, Tuesday.

Will I accidentally mix bleach and ammonia?

I breathed a sigh of relief when he came home, everything smelled and looked like it had been worn—ketchup stains and all—and I felt a tinge of success. That was up until the time that I saw a friend who had been on the campus that same time.

"I saw Abram on campus about a month ago."

"Oh yeah, he had a little chance to visit with the big boys."

"Yeah, I'm not sure what all they were involved in—some kind of game, I guess. I just remember he had his shirt inside out, and he had a piece of tape on his back that said Tuesday. I thought that was kind of strange since it was Saturday."

Case in point. Kids will be kids. Moms, do what you can, and don't worry, if it's not a matter of salvation. We've heard it more times than we care to: Don't sweat the small stuff. But what about the big stuff?

> *But the Lord answered her, "Martha, Martha, you are anxious and troubled about many things, but one thing is necessary. Mary has chosen the good portion, which will not be taken away from her"*
> *(Luke 10:41–42).*

Sweating the Big Stuff

Let me share a case of *worryitis extraordinaire*. We lived in south Mississippi. With four small kids in tow, we decided to take a day off and head to the river. We crossed into Louisiana territory, and just before reaching our destination, we stopped at a gas station, quickly filled up, and then back on the road to the Tangipahoa River. Upon arrival, we parked, began unstrapping kids, unpacking the cooler, answering a lot of questions, and then reached for hands to hold as we strolled down to the waterfront, but we were minus two hands. The one-year-old was there, as were the four-year-old and the seven-year-old, but the five-year-old was nowhere to be seen. Onset of worry. Frenzy of running, calling, and flailing of limbs. Panic had to give way to planning. That was imperative. I would stay at the river, and my husband would make a mad dash back to the gas station.

Look at the birds of the air.

We had one cell phone between us in those days, and there was no such thing as data. So I didn't know. I didn't know that when he reached the gas station there was no sign of her. Outside. I didn't know that when he went inside, she was sitting high on the counter with her legs swinging three feet off the floor. I didn't know she was chewing a candy bar and being promised by a team of admirers that we would be back for her.

I didn't know. So I was worried. Was it okay? Was it okay to sweat then, since it was the big stuff I was sweating?

I probably can't make a legal argument for it, but I think so. Here's why. It's a different brand of worry. I was too busy praying, really, to talk myself into fretting. And while I was praying, I was searching. Did anyone see a little girl? Did anyone see any movement in the water? Was there anything tall enough that she could be behind it without my seeing her? Were there small footprints anywhere on the shore? It was the desperate searching of a desperate soul.

The "Don't Worry" Verses

The first kind of worry, "small stuff" worry—Will my son have enough clothes to wear?—violated the don't-worry verses more literally than any example I can think of. Turn to Matthew 6:

> Therefore I tell you, do not be anxious about your life, what you will eat or what you will drink, nor about your body, what you will put on. Is not life more than food, and the body more than clothing? Look at the birds of the air: they neither sow nor reap nor gather into barns, and yet your heavenly Father feeds them. Are you not of more value than they? And which of you by being anxious can add a single hour to his span of life? And why are you anxious about clothing? Consider the lilies of the field, how they grow: they neither toil nor spin, yet I tell you, even Solomon in all his glory was not arrayed like one of these. But if God so clothes the grass of the field, which today is alive and tomorrow is thrown into the oven, will he not much more clothe you, O you of little faith? Therefore do not be anxious, saying, "What shall we eat?" or "What shall we drink?" or "What shall we wear?" For the Gentiles seek after these things, and your heavenly Father knows that you need them all (Matt. 6:25–32).

I was worried. I was worried about what he would put on. Shame on me. All it takes is a glance at the meadow to know this is of no consequence whatsoever. It's against the background of the verses above that a more familiar one emerges next. "But seek first the kingdom of God and his righteousness, and all these things will be added to you" (v. 33).

No worries. We sing that verse a lot at devotionals, don't we? And we can sing "Seek ye first" pretty loud as long as we know, deep down, we really mean second.

The context is your next meal, your next pair of blue jeans, and your next cup of coffee. And Jesus spends a somewhat lengthy oration here addressing the issue. You think he wanted to make it clear to a people who can get really caught up in thinking about life's essentials? I mean, they're called essentials for a reason, right?

Peace Over Worry

The real issue here is not really an empty glass or a full glass, but it's about faith. How do you show your faith? How do you strengthen it? How do you solidify it? You don't worry. Even when it comes to putting food on the table, if it interferes in any way with seeking God and his righteousness, don't do it. Wait. What? Don't put food on the table? Are you out of your mind?

No, not yet! But peace over worry is of the even-if and no-matter-what caliber. The Word of God promises us that if we will keep the goal of seeking him first, we can rest assured he's going to do the adding. And God can do the math. When he serves the dinner, you never run out of food (Mark 8:19–20; Exod. 16:35; 1 Kings 17:14–15; 2 Kings 4:3–4). As the psalmist said, "I have been young, and now am old, yet I have not seen the righteous forsaken or his children begging for bread" (Ps. 37:25).

These passages do not teach us to have a lackadaisical attitude in the midst of true crisis, but it is reiterated several times in these verses that when it comes to what you're going to eat, what you're going to drink, and what you're going to wear, God always has and always will provide for his beloved children. Any time we find ourselves questioning how, it is just a test of our trust in him. Ace the test! Verse 33 is pass or fail.

> The wicked watches for the righteous and seeks to put him to death. The Lord will not abandon him to his power or let him be condemned when he is brought to trial (Ps. 37:32–33).

Was Jesus Worried?

But what about that second kind of "big stuff" worry? The one where a child is missing. The gamut of "missing" is a big one. It includes the incident at the river bank and gas station. It includes the child who is struggling with self. It includes the child who is not quite the same one he was yesterday, whose joy has withdrawn so much the parents are trying to reach deep within him to help retrieve it. The infant and the adult. The one whose health has brought you to your knees or the one whose soul has kept you there. Missing. Lost. It stirs the heart of God in heaven and brings him down to earth. "For the Son of Man came to seek and to save the lost" (Luke 19:10).

If God's heart is stirred this deeply over the lost, don't think it's wrong for yours to be. Yes, it's okay to sweat the big stuff, as long as that sweat is accompanied by prayer, trust, and obedience. I don't intend for this to have the slightest tinge of flippancy, but truly, more vividly than any man-made illustration, Jesus our Savior sweated the big stuff. "And being in agony he prayed more earnestly; and his sweat became like great drops of blood falling down to the ground" (Luke 22:44). His prayer was earnest, more earnest even than it had been before. His trust was full, with his "nevertheless" plea. "Father, if you are willing, remove this cup from me. Nevertheless, not my will, but yours, be done" (v. 42). He was obedient to death (Phil. 2:8).

Let not your hearts be troubled, neither let them be afraid (John 14:27).

Troubled Hearts Banned

But even in the face of the big stuff, even in sweat beads, Christ wants a calm for us. Jesus' words to those on the brink of desperation are sweeter than a caramel latte. John 14 begins with "Let not your hearts be troubled." It's enticing advice, but how do we get there? How do we relax a heart that's ready to burst out of the chest in worry? Read on. Jesus doesn't leave us hanging. "You believe in God; believe also in me." That's it. In eight words, we have the entire thesis, discussion, and conclusion. Jesus says something else toward the end of the chapter that's also interesting: "Let not your hearts be troubled" (v. 27). Wait, that was back in verse 1, right? Right. But he says it twice. That doubles the importance in my mind.

Isn't *twice* significant? Think of how we use it. Did you check to make sure you blew out all the scented candles before leaving the house? Twice. Have you seen the new Batman movie? Twice. Did you stop and get coffee on the way? Twice.

Twice is always a short way of saying, "Oh yes, this is super important to me!" What's super important to Jesus? That his followers not have troubled hearts. Don't get it backwards. We often do. We somehow feel we are more pleasing to God if we stay upset because of the enemy's tactics when in reality Jesus said twice, "Let not your hearts be troubled." And that was with the crucifixion looming in close proximity.

What's super important to Jesus?

The second "Let not your hearts be troubled" is on the heels of this assurance: "Peace I leave with you; my peace I give to you. Not as the world gives do I give to you."

The world's peace is contingent on surrounding circumstances. Christ's peace for his followers is not. We don't wait for the six o'clock news to tell us whether we have peace. We don't base peace on which brother-in-law shows up for Thanksgiving dinner.

And so as I paced the waterfront calling "Mattianne" over the roar of the boats and the chop of the river, it was the desperate search of a desperate soul. Every beat of my heart spelled out, "God help me." I believe there is more reliance than worry in that oneness. The idea that I can have an open conversation with the Helper in times of trouble (Ps. 46:1) and that he cares and hears (Ps. 34:4) expels the worry and brings focus to the situation. I was knocking, I was certainly asking, and you better believe I was seeking (Matt. 7:7).

Things don't always wrap up as neatly as they did at the end of that day. For sure. At least here on earth. Christ's prayer for there to be another way if possible did not take him away from the cross or its cruelty. But the prayer was answered. God's will was done. Praise God! His will was done.

"Do not be anxious about anything," Philippians 4:6 tells us. I heard the same thing from a five-year-old boy a while back, only he phrased it slightly different: "I ain't afraid o'nothin'!"

Not so with the world. There are a lot of phobias out there, including anatidaephobia, which is the fear of ducks. As I understand it, this phobia is specifically about the fear that a duck is actually somewhere watching the individual at all times. There is also sidonglobophobia, the fear of cotton balls, and bananaphobia. Figure it out. I'm pretty sure I have a phobia of having any of these words on a spelling test.

As ludicrous as some of these sound, and I'm not making fun of those who are troubled by these thoughts, there are hundreds and hundreds of these irrational fears. Think about it. If you are a child of God, every single fear is an irrational one.

Psalm 46:2 says, "Therefore we will not fear though the earth gives way, though the mountains be moved into the heart of the sea." Um, that's a description of something that might get your adrenaline going just a little. But there's a "therefore" at the beginning of that sentence, and whatever comes before it indicates the reason for the truth after it. Verse 1: "God is our refuge and strength, a very present help in trouble." For that reason, verse 2. Is the earth about to collapse? Are the mountains packing for a cruise? Bring it! God is a very present help in trouble.

"I ain't afraid o'nothin'!"

Before Charles Dickens forever married the word "Ebenezer" to Christmas visions that weren't exactly sugar plums dancing, the name truly meant something precious. In 1 Samuel 7, we read the people were afraid of the Philistines. What? When God was on their side? That was before the thunder. At the sound of the Lord's thunder, the Philistines broke into confusion, and they were defeated. "Then Samuel took a stone and set it up between Mizpah and Shen and called its name Ebenezer; for he said, 'Till now the Lord has helped us.'" Hasn't he? What are we worried about?

Big stuff, small stuff, in-between stuff. Matthew 6 says we can't do a thing about it. We can't make ourselves a bit taller, though women are notorious for trying. If we can't get a few inches by putting a spike on the heel of our shoes, we'll bouff up our hair until the bride of Frankenstein has nothing on us.

We have to face it. There are some things we just can't help.

Don't worry. Be happy. Ebenezer.

> *Casting all your anxieties on him,*
> *because he cares for you*
> *(1 Pet. 5:7).*

If You're Happy, You Will Know It

1. Do you agree with the statement, "If you are a child of God, every single fear is an irrational one"? Why or why not?

2. For fun, look up a list of phobias on the internet. Which ones describe truly fearful situations, and which ones are just imagined danger?

3. Earlier, I failed to say that the five-year-old who said, "I ain't afraid o' nothin'" suddenly had a snake fall from a tree into his path the moment he finished that statement, and he ran off screaming like a fox in mating season. How do we quote scripture concerning being fearless because of faith in God, and then sometimes immediately show a lack of faith when "the snakes begin to fall"? Discuss specific examples either in scripture or in your life.

4. In our society, we sometimes view the helper as a less important assistant to the one who's really in charge. Our God does not fit this concept. A better illustration is a person calling out desperately for help, and when the help comes, it is a qualified responder who makes a rescue, without which the person would not have survived. With that in mind, look for other verses not in this chapter that refer to God as a help or helper. Now look at the context of that name. How desperate are the circumstances?

Happy Trails

And speaking of Preparation-H and other over-the-counter solutions . . .

Where would we be without them? I, for one, am glad for the invention of the medicine cabinet because we can quickly access critically needed items such as cotton swabs, lip balm, and the cord to an electric razor no one has seen since 1998.

We do keep a stash of over-the-counters handy just in case they're needed. These meds are located just behind the towels in the linen closet and under the humidifier and heating pad. So in case of an emergency, the infirmed person is heard saying, "Yeah, scoot that thing over, and there's a bottle of Tylenol in that little plastic box with the ... no under that; the green one. Yes, it has a sticker on it that says 'Clinton/Gore,' but never mind now. I think the incubation period has passed, and I'm pretty recovered in here."

To which the searcher responds, "Oh good, whew, I need two of these aspirin after pulling all this stuff out of the linen closet."

It's even harder to find a Band-Aid. The more blood that's flowing, the more difficult the task. My husband showed up to preach one Sunday with a Barbie Band-Aid around his thumb.

Medicines have been a part of life on earth since Eve kept Adam up all night with a coughing fit, but there are basically three schools of thought about them: (1) Take the medicine; (2) Don't take the medicine; (3) Eat tree bark.

And when it comes to schools of thought, that last one is a 7A school with four annexes. Everybody is jumping on the natural healing band-wagon. I have a friend who's all about it. We were eating lunch together one day, and I don't have the greatest focus in conversation anyway. So we're sitting there eating lunch talking about normal stuff like—I don't know—bad referee calls and even worse fashion trends, when suddenly, with no warning, she pops a dandelion in her mouth, chews it, and swallows. She did. I have no recollection of anything that was said in the conversation after that. All I could think was, "Did you just . . .?"

So as you can imagine, she has a real knack for knowing what natural resources can be used for health benefits. And right now, among those resources, coconut oil is a biggie. I wish I could grow a coconut tree on my patio. I could pay off my house and yours with the proceeds. It's now being used to heal insect bites, indigestion, constipation, warts, and occasional rabies. I'm pretty sure my friend is putting it directly on her armpits to immediately capture and destroy any unexpected sweat.

Some of my girlfriends vow that it enhances memory. It might. I'm not saying it doesn't. In fact, I can't remember what I was saying. Pass the coconut oil.

Oh yeah, so my dad had become a little forgetful in the last few months of his life. Since we didn't think it could hurt and it could possibly help, we were mixing coconut oil into all four food groups. For him, that was root beer, candied orange slices, peanuts, and cheese-flavored chips. Um, now that I just typed that, I'm thinking there might have been a health issue here greater than the memory one.

My sister brought up that maybe we could check into the memory aid that was being advertised on TV. You know, the one that works due to an ingredient originally found in jellyfish? That claim gives me pause. I mean, are jellyfish known for being particularly stellar in the area of memory? Do they say, "Hey, I remember this leg. I stung it back in the Spring Break of 2012"?

I find that, by and large, a lot of people are putting supplements on their supplements, and I guess that's why we need supplemental health insurance. Can't we just go back to the Flintstones vitamins? I mean, those things tasted good, and as long as we were eating them, we could climb three trees and ride our bike around the block all between the time our mother called us for supper and the time she called us by our first, middle, and last name for supper. We were healthy! So while the medical world is saying coconut oil and elderberry juice and research shows improvement in studies where among males with no prior etcetera, etcetera; I say Yabba Dabba Doo!

Yeah, go with vitamins! Although to be honest, I'm even a little hesitant there. We're entrusting our health to these things produced by people who can't spell or count. I mean there are like twelve B vitamins named riboflavin, folic acid, thiamine, etc. Do you notice something? Not a single one of them start with the letter B. Not one. And most of the time we skip from vitamin B8 to B12. I mean I know 9, 10, and 11 exist, but they don't get a fair shake. Who really ever heard of B11? Who? And K stands for potassium and vitamin H is biotin. There's a B in that word, people. Did it not occur to you when you were deciding who could get in the B clan? I know, I know; it's complex. But it just seems to me that most of the people who are walking the halls of the medical summit never once took a walk down Sesame Street.

Before you badger me too much, let me say I'm for it. I'm all in. Give me natural healing—especially seeing that the date on the medicine bottle was about the time Tennessee won a national championship, some of the medicines out there cost more than my first car, and it's a twenty-minute drive to the pharmacy. With these considerations in mind, there are dandelions shooting up in my front yard, and they are free for the taking.

Originally printed in Christian Woman *magazine, January/February 2020.*

IF MAMA AIN'T HAPPY,
Take Her to the Mountain

Circumstances or Substance

Six-year-old boys can get away with wearing bright colorful pants on Easter. Not that they want to. They'd much rather have on a Batman cape and a pair of mismatched socks that would slide enough on linoleum to make a grand entrance. But moms tend to push for pretty pants.

I was part of a poll one Easter weekend. A snaggle-toothed boy I had never seen before came up to me and asked if I liked his pastel pink pants. "Oh, I love them," I said, delighted to have been asked.

That was not the result he was hoping for, as he was obviously trying to get the masses to vote against his mom. He hit his forehead with the palm of his hand, and looked at my husband. "What about him? Does *he* like them?"

A couple of hours later, we were near a beautiful fountain surrounded by Easter lilies. And mothers with cameras. And tired children in pastel pants. Families were taking turns getting the required picture to post for the world to see. Most of them were miserable failures at this point. Oh, the parents with only one kid were doing okay, even though the expressions they captured pretty much communicated the kid must be sitting in poison oak. But put one, two, or in one case six siblings in the photo session, and the "Thirty Years' War" suddenly gets condensed into twenty horrible seconds. I heard a lot of bribes from the parents going on, followed by a lot of threats. And then it happened. One of the best moments of my life.

A six-year-old boy with flaming red hair and in adorable green pants began to shift on an unsteady rock on the fountain wall, and before his mother could say Jack Robinson or Ralph Lauren, there was a splash. I don't know what they did with their camera, but I grabbed mine in record time.

The child was both drenched and terrified, the siblings overjoyed, the mother did a sudden live demonstration of the entire history of the Red Cross, but the words of the husband crowned the whole thing, "I hope you're happy!"

Of course, these four words mean, "I'm pretty sure you're not, but since you made the rest of us miserable so you could accomplish your goal, we're getting a tiny bit of satisfaction right now."

Don't lie; you've been there too.

There's No "If" in Happiness

We fool ourselves into thinking if we can accomplish some feat such as taking a family picture with all eyes on the camera, all lips turned upward, and all tongues caged; if we can acquire some wanted item; if we can get something that will ease our work load; if our pillow can be a little fluffier and our puppy a little more continent, we'll achieve the H-goal. We'll be happy!

It's not that any of these things aren't good within themselves—go for them! Just understand they will not bring happiness. If physical conditions could determine happiness, here's what it would be. For me, I would say happiness is . . .

○ Opening the dryer to find that all the socks have happily stayed with their partners through the entire cycle.

○ Accidentally dropping an iron skillet on all nine of the Star Wars Saga DVDs.

○ Taking off your bra at the end of the day . . . or anytime.

○ Going to Chuck E. Cheese to find that none of the sound effects on any of the games are working.

○ Going to the Dollar Tree without spending forty.

○ Going to the VBS meeting and finding out that all the craft positions have been snatched up.

○ Discovering that your family has one too few tickets to the wrestling match.

○ Finding out that fried foods boost the immune system and aid in digestion.

○ Dusty blinds becoming all the rage.

○ A power failure during election returns.

○ Finding out that empty ice cream pails are selling for a fortune on eBay.

○ Learning that the dirty Santa game has been banned from all future church Christmas parties.

○ Getting legislation passed that the parents no longer have to be in the front seat when a teenager is learning to drive . . . or the back seat . . . or in the car at all.

○ Pre-washed turnip greens.

○ Everyone agreeing to watch Andy Griffith instead of NASCAR.

○ Your disposable toilet seat liner not getting automatically flushed before you sit on it.

Yeah, that's my list, but the truth is, happiness simply does not come about from a set of circumstances; it comes from a condition of the soul.

Blessed Thoughts

Jesus had a seat on the side of the mountain and forever answered the question of how to be happy in Matthew 5. We refer to these scriptures as the beatitudes. It's a man-made name, and most of us would be hard-pressed to provide a definition of it. But Jesus begins to list the "blessed are" contingencies.

Let's look at that word: blessed. In this passage, it is translated from the Greek word *makarioi*. It instantly makes me think of macaroni, which is a pretty blessed thought. But the same word is used in some fifty New Testament passages, and in several of them, depending on the translation, it reads "happy." John 13:17, for starters, reads "If ye know these things, happy (*makarioi*) are ye if ye do them" (KJV). In Acts 26:2, Paul says, "I think myself happy (*makariou*), king Agrippa" (KJV). And in Romans 14:22 "happy" describes the who does not condemn himself in what he eats. It's that same Greek word again.

"I think myself happy, king Agrippa."

—Paul

I have heard a number of people say that Jesus never promised his followers happiness. I beg to differ! From the side of a mountain, he gave the first seminar and one often quoted on how to be happy. In a world where the pursuit of happiness is a phrase in the very founding document of our nation, where advertisers sell its promise in three easy payments, and where one phrase is repeated from the homeless camps to the Hollywood mansions, "I just want to be happy," Jesus tells us how. But it's not what you would guess.

By all means, if we can learn how to be happy from the words of the one who knows how, if he thought it important enough to perch himself in human form on the side of a mountain and lay it out for us, let's get front row seats. Let's plug this passage into the memory verse chart for our children first. That will save them a lot of heartache in looking in all the wrong places for the rest of their lives.

> *Blessed are the poor in spirit, for theirs is the kingdom of heaven (Matt. 5:3).*

Poor in Spirit

We begin with verse 3 of Matthew 5. "Blessed are the poor in spirit, for theirs is the kingdom of heaven." I've heard quite a few discourses through the years concerning what "poor in spirit" means here. Is it really that hard to grasp? I'm going to go out on a limb and say it means poor in spirit. We've all heard people answer "poorly" when we ask how they're doing, and we usually try to make a quick getaway before we hear all the details. That could be an answer to physical well-being though, so Jesus clarifies that this is emotional. We're poor in spirit. We're just sad sometimes. It happens. It should not have taken a Pixar movie to key us in to the secret that joy and sadness are connected. Jesus does it here. Happy are you when you're sad? If you're puzzled, you should be. It takes the rest of the "beatitude" for it to make sense. In fact, it's true across the board.

> Happy are you when you're sad?

All of these "Happy are you" statements are contingent on the end of the statement being true. I can make it through part A, a difficulty, with happiness, joy, and blessedness because I know beyond a shadow of a doubt, part B. What is part B? "For yours is the kingdom of heaven." There is no difficulty that can challenge that or make it untrue. There is no sadness in my life that is not overridden by the fact that I'm going to heaven. Sad? Yeah, at times, but the ultimate reality is I'm going to heaven. The big picture is, I'm happy.

Those Who Mourn

The second statement is my favorite, but it hasn't always been. "Blessed are those who mourn." There would have to be something wrong with a person who found joy in that. But the rest of the statement says, "for they shall be comforted." That makes us feel a little better. Mourning is hard. Grieving over a loss is one of the most helpless feelings we can experience. There is nothing we can do to reverse the situation. That, paired with the close attachment we had to the person we loved so deeply, now gone, makes the pain cut to the core of our being.

But there is also a comfort. I remember after the first blow of hearing my dad had departed this life, even though I knew it was coming, after the numbness, the reality of where he was occurred to me. When I thought about the things he was experiencing at that moment, a euphoria engulfed me. For the Christian, there is one aspiration that dims all the others. When that dream is realized, victory! Celebration! Beyond the idea of conquering (Rom. 8:37)! "Oh death, where is your victory? Oh death, where is your sting?" (1 Cor. 15:55). "Precious in the sight of the Lord is the death of his saints" (Ps. 116:15).

For as great as this idea is, I think there is another level of meaning to Jesus' words because I think there is a mourning that even supersedes that at funerals. Is there something sadder than death? Is there a mourning over greater heartache and damage? There is. The path of destruction brought about by my own sin is devastating. There is nothing else that comes close to sin's wasteland. What started with desire has brought about its wages. Some compound sin with more sin, some run, some hide, some try to cover it with lies or laughter. Oh, but some mourn. And God assures us a way to reckon with our sins when we do. What on earth or in heaven could be more beautiful than washing them away, as described in Acts 22:16? Or what catharsis could be imagined to be more comforting than the already baptized Christian confessing sin and being healed (1 John 1:9)? "Blessed are those who mourn, for they shall be comforted." Yes, it is my favorite.

Which, of all these scenarios in the mountainside list, makes your happy list? Not one, at first glance. They're all bummers. This is not just a list of attitudes we're supposed to have, but more a list of attributes that rise to the occasion in the most grueling of circumstances that, by and large, we can't help.

Blessed are the meek, for they shall inherit the earth (Matt. 5:5).

The Meek

The next one is "Blessed are the meek, for they shall inherit the earth." This is sometimes mistaken for "Blessed are the mousey." Jesus described himself as meek and lowly, but no one could describe him as mousey. The word has to do with accepting humble circumstances, such as a manger, a sacrifice of doves, and no place to lay your head. In fact, the Greek word here is translated *humble* in Matthew 21:5, "Behold, your king is coming to you, humble, and mounted on a donkey." Where those of the world get what they think they want by railroading through, this kind of meekness and gentleness puts the welfare of others first. It's scarce in our society.

No matter how many times we hear "I'm humbled to receive this award," that's kind of paradoxical to even put those things in the same sentence. Receiving awards is popular, but receiving humbling circumstances is not. Meekness is a degree of maturity we strive to reach in our spiritual journey, and we usually get there incrementally. The world doesn't get it. At all. Why would someone want others to succeed over themselves? Why would we like serving over being served? Why would we rather mop the floor than floor the mob? Because we are becoming like Jesus, and we've chosen to forfeit, at times, material desires, status, luxury, or comfort for meekness. What's happy about that? It's a loss—whether financial or prestige, and we find that this game we're playing has a lot more chutes than ladders.

Jesus talks about this kind of loss in Matthew 10:39. You lose, you win. How? How can I have happiness by losing out on so much? Think of what you're getting: "For they shall inherit the earth." I'm pretty sure it's not the third-rock-from-the-sun earth. That one has a lot of problems, and I'm not interested in bidding on it. Peter said it's going to be dissolved (2 Pet. 3:11), so that would not be a good deal.

However, Revelation 21 describes a new earth prepared especially for this inheritance (Rev. 21:3; John 14:2). It makes every act of submission and meekness

> Is there something sadder than death?

a greater deposit toward happiness, when we realize this earth has no tears or death (Rev. 21:4). Happy!

Those Who Hunger and Thirst after Righteousness

These happiness-in-spite-of—even because of—adversity beatitudes continue. After all, when do we most hunger for righteousness? When are we most keyed in on God and his will? It's when we're hurting the most. There's happiness in hurting the most, because of the tagline: you'll be filled.

The Merciful

And mercy. Mercy is a beautiful thing, but it's not invited to the party until things get really vile and ugly. That's when mercy is most needed. And we, the hurt, extend it and find amazing peace and joy in it, as we realize how deeply we depend on it for our life, our soul, our salvation.

The Pure in Heart

The pure in heart, next on the list, are happy. Sure they're happy! You never regret doing the right thing because, at your very heart, you want an unadulterated relationship with God. But you're going to miss some things, because they're just not pure. They may be inviting, and promise the very happiness we think we'd like to embrace, but they're not the pure choice. You may miss the prom, the office party, the senior trip, or the top movie of the year. But you're going to see something better. Jesus reminds us, and never let us forget it for one second, we're going to see God.

The Peacemakers

The peacemakers? Oh no! If you need to be a peacemaker, that can only mean one thing. There is trouble, and it's probably in the form of bickering, hurt feelings, and jealousy, and it is on the verge of escalating to worse. It in no form resembles happiness. But again, Jesus shows us the joy worth the pain. What can be better than being called the children of God?

Children, for the most part, look like their parents. We went to the Founder's Day celebration in Killen, Alabama, once. Yeah, I wondered who named the town too. I mean, if you say it out loud, it sounds like there's been a tragedy. But we didn't go for the town; we went for the granny. Because they couldn't find anyone older than my husband's grandmother, she was the Grand Marshall for the Founder's Day parade. It was a small town, and my husband's mother had grown up there. Her maiden name was Myra Wallace.

As we were standing waiting for the festivities to start, and not sure if they had already, someone took a look at my toddler, and said, "I don't know who that child is, but one thing's for sure, she's got to be Myra Wallace's granddaughter because she looks just like her."

There is a sense in which I can look like God.

It's possible for people to look at you, even when they don't know you, and think of your parents. Why? Because you look just like them. When we're peacemakers, we look like our Father. As worthless and vile as I have been in the past, as much as I am a forgiven sinner, in the middle of a tough situation, when I navigate peace instead of stirring the trouble, there is a sense in which I can look like God. It's almost unfathomable, but Jesus says it, and it certainly is a happy realization.

After all, God is all about peace. From Genesis to Revelation, his story is a story of peace. It's all about reconciling man to God. God came down to earth to restore peace (Col. 1:20). All enduring happiness lies within that premise.

Those Who Are Persecuted for Righteousness' Sake

While my favorite one is "those who mourn," the most astounding one, the one Jesus spends the most time on and ensures we understand, is the last one.

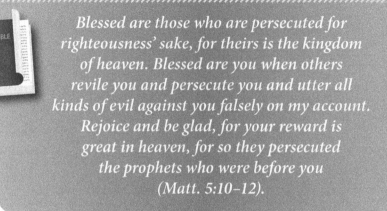

Blessed are those who are persecuted for righteousness' sake, for theirs is the kingdom of heaven. Blessed are you when others revile you and persecute you and utter all kinds of evil against you falsely on my account. Rejoice and be glad, for your reward is great in heaven, for so they persecuted the prophets who were before you (Matt. 5:10–12).

When we're persecuted, we react in a number of ways, and one of them is generally not rejoicing. We may cry, yell, fume, call our senator, or write a "call to action" in a bulletin or gospel publication. We generally repeat one phrase, "It's scary!" This phrase is in complete contradiction to what scriptures repeatedly tell us, "Do not fear."

In fact, be glad. The word translated "glad" in verse 12 is, in some translations, "exceedingly glad." It carries a higher degree of joy than your ordinary passed-a-chemistry-final glad. That's why in other cases, and in various translations of scripture, the Greek word is rendered "rejoiced greatly" (Acts 16:34; 1 Pet. 1:6, 8) and "exceeding joy" (1 Pet. 4:13 NKJV).

Take a minute and let that sink in. I think it takes more than a minute for most of us. It took more than that for the audience on the mountain.

Fast forward to Acts 5. The apostles found themselves persecuted, and it wasn't just by a couple of haters. It was the high priest, and all who were with him (the party of the Sadducees) (v. 17). And they weren't just given a fine; they were thrown into prison. But there's not a jail cell an angel couldn't open, if it was God's doing—and it was (v. 19). After their miraculous release, events progressed quickly, the apostles would not agree to the strict charge to be silent about Jesus (v. 28) but simply said, "We must obey God rather than men" (v. 29). We are told the council wanted to kill the apostles at this point, but instead, they beat them, threatened them, and released them.

We don't read of them screaming "Unfair!" They didn't throw a pity party, and no one was shaking in their sandals. We do read, "Then they left the presence of the council, rejoicing that they were counted worthy to suffer dishonor for the name" (Acts 5:41). I believe it had sunk in. I believe they made a connection to what they heard on the side of the mountain from the lips of the very one they were determined to teach about.

I believe we should too. To sum it up, be happy!

Even if your green pants get drenched.

> *They left . . . rejoicing that they were counted worthy to suffer dishonor for the name*
> *(Acts 5:41).*

If You're Happy, You Will Know It

1. What is your take on "Blessed are those who mourn"? Do you think its meaning is primarily about grief over death of a loved one? Does the other explanation seem more or less plausible, and why?

2. When we take it to mean death of a loved one, it is easy to see the fact that we will be comforted when we are Christians, and the loved ones are Christians. It's more difficult to find comfort when our loved ones, who are not Christians, die. Assuming this mourning is about death, how, from your own experience or others you know, are we comforted as Christians even in these circumstances?

3. What verse most comforts you when you are grieving? Which song in our song books?

4. Think of a person who is mourning death. Do something special for her this week. Either send her a special memory you had of her loved one, find a picture of the person and put an encouraging note with it, or just say, "Let's go out to eat or to a movie."

5. Now think of a person mourning sin. Do something special for her this week. Send a note or text with a favorite Bible verse of encouragement. Tell her "I just prayed for you, and I'm doing it every day." If you have time for another "Let's go out to eat," by all means, she could use the friendship right now!

6. These "happy are you when" passages are hard to swallow for adults. Do you agree that they can be helpful to the life of a child who memorizes them? It takes some maturity and life experience to grasp a greater meaning, but how can we feed them to our children in ways they can understand?

7. Do a study of *makari* in all its forms in the New Testament. Consult an English/Greek concordance or Biblehub.com. Write down your favorite use of it, and beside it write the succinct definition you think the word communicates in that passage.

8. Read Matthew 10:39. What does this mean? Can you think of specific cases where a loss means a gain?

Happy Trails

And speaking of granddaughters . . .

It changes things. One only needs to read through the book of Ruth to see it's true. In chapter 1, Naomi is shouting "unfair," and renaming herself "Bitter." Plot twist. Spoiler alert. Grandchild arrives in three chapters, and she's suddenly praising the Lord with a baby on her lap.

Something apparently happens outside the birthing room when something happens in it. While the mother is gritting her teeth and twisting her husband's wrist out of socket, a change comes over one woman waiting in the lobby. Whereas just a few moments ago, she was still the mother, worrying if the blankets were sanitary, if the doctor had enough initials after his name, and counting the pairs of clean under-wear in the suitcase, now in an instant she has become Naomi—in the after pictures.

She takes one look and a hundred and forty-two pictures of the shriv-eled up new life, and then races to Walmart to pick out a swing set. She has suddenly become less about clean underwear and more about tutus and makeshift superhero capes from dish towels and clothespins.

In a couple of years, the woman who used to be so straight-laced she wouldn't step out of the house without a monogrammed rain bonnet in tow, afraid someone would see a hair out of place, is now racing a kid down the grocery store sidewalk on an air motorcycle going "Bood'n, bood'n!" And winning!

Her discipline tactics have gone out the window. It's kind of frustrat-ing that we walked a line so tight it snapped in a couple of places, and now the line has widened so much that the boot camp has now become a party.

Where we were told, "You are not walking out of this house dressed like that," our kids are told, "Hang on, sweet pea, let me whip out my sew-ing machine and make you a hobo bag to match your shredded jeans."

And while, if someone had approached our parents with something like, "I hate to be the one to tell you, but your child threw a piece of ice at the fellowship meal, and it hit someone in the head," they would respond with, "How dare you insinuate that my child would be involved in that kind of behavior," the grandparents instead respond with, "I *know!* Isn't it *great?* That kid is a hoot!"

On September 8 we celebrate her. And him. For all the frivolity of Grandmother, Grandpa ups the ante. Our friend James chased a train across two states until he ran out of gas because his grandson didn't want the choo-choo to leave.

And what about your grandpa? What about mine? I realize now that in my youngest years he still held a demanding job and tended a mas-sive garden as well as shepherding a flock at church. Apparently none of that got in the way of loading me up in the truck and heading for the mountains. We made cups out of leaves and drank from the spring, and I remember thinking, "We should have brought cups from that cabinet at your house; they work better." He showed me periwinkles, which sounded a lot like my favorite cartoon character Bullwinkle, and looked a lot like raisins, so I downed them before he could stop me. It was too late when I learned they were snails, and he laughed like crazy, because you know, grandparents kind of are. Hey, I was doing escargot before my friends could even spell it (which is probably still the case). He let me have his dolly—not the kind with googly eyes and a frilly dress, but the kind made out of a pallet and four wheels—and I cruised down a steep incline in the middle of the street.

Yeah, I'd say grandparents pretty much lose their minds. That's why they can draw kids to them like nerds to Atari-fest. I made the mistake of sending my kids to a college where the grandparents live halfway between the college and our house. I remember that first free weekend when my child was planning to come home. I tidied up her room, lit her favorite candle, and made sure I had a few of her favorite snacks on hand. I could hardly wait to hear about all of her college adventures.

I did the mileage in my head and knew what time her Friday class dismissed. It was almost time for the front door to open. But it didn't. The minute hand took a few trips around the dial, darkness set in, and still no headlights climbed the drive. I finally made a frantic call, "Are you okay? Did your car break down? How many pairs of clean underwear did you pack?"

"Huh?" came the answer. "I stopped at Grandmyra's. We've been at the Cracker Barrel. We're about to bake cookies. Then we're going to watch all 180 episodes of *I Love Lucy*."

I've accepted it. What is here to compete with the free-for-all at Grandmyra's? I'll see my daughter at graduation.

Yes, it's almost National Grandparents Day. Hats off to all grandmothers and grandfathers. Salute. Thanks for being there when we need you. And should our kids ever tire of endless cookies and wheelies on the deck, driving—yes, driving—in your lap through the field of cows who are dodging the swerving Oldsmobile, send our charges back our way. We the parents, who still have our minds, will be waiting. With fresh veggies and stacks of clean underwear

Originally printed in Christian Woman *magazine, September/October 2019.*

3

IF MAMA AIN'T HAPPY,
Get Her a Towel: That Cup's Running Over!
Bummed or Blessed

My dad always told the four of us that we thought the law of gravity had been repealed. It's because we would be careless with our glass of juice or milk or some other liquid by setting it half on a piece of furniture and half off, or brushing it with our arm when the missile (formerly known as a spoon) was making an emergency crash landing into the ocean of Fruit Loops. We learned that the law of gravity was still in effect, and what we couldn't get with our sister's sleeve, we took care of by running to get the best dish towel. Our cup was overflowing.

Proverbially, and I suppose originally from Psalm 23:5, an overflowing cup is a symbol of tremendous blessings. It just so happens that most of the time when our cup is overflowing, we're not paying a bit of attention to the pouring. Is that a parallel or what?

> *You prepare a table before me in the presence of my enemies; you anoint my head with oil; my cup overflows (Ps. 23:5).*

The Great Pourer and Preparer

We gripe about the weather and the football score, all the time not even realizing that the Pourer is streaming more blessings into our container than we can realize or hold. We memorize Psalm 23 in the primary grades—well, we used to—and then it sits on the back burner of our heart until we stand by an open grave. It's a good place to remember it because it takes us through the part about the valley of the shadow of death, but there's so much more there about life.

Back it up to verse 1. "The Lord is my shepherd; I shall not want." Discussion over. Case closed. We could end a discussion of happiness right here, but if you know me, you probably know I'm not finished. It was just today that, on the way to worship, my son made a comment from the back seat, saying that was his two cents, and then I added to the discussion after which my husband said, "I think we're up to fifty-two cents now." So yeah, let's keep going.

We get to this cup part in verse 5, and there's so much more than the cup. There's a whole table! And the table must be incredibly furnished because it has been prepared by the Great Preparer. I've seen some tables at Thanksgiving and fifth-Sunday fellowships that make me ashamed at the amount that's furnished. We're above the legal limit on turnip greens, and the dessert table puts us in a coma just looking at it. Everything in that corner that isn't walking around is covered with meringue. We're stuffed more than the eggs were. Put that side by side with the Super Bowl table at my house once a year, and it looks like a pack of Lunchables. We've got chicken with bigger fingers than wings (also there) and pigs popping out of their blankets faster than Usain Bolt on caffeine.

We're grand preparers in the Lord's church. We *think* we are. Can you imagine how measly our meals look, how measly even a meal in Windsor Castle or the White House would look compared to one prepared by God Almighty, Creator of the universe, Founder of the feast? Go get a towel! Your cup's running over.

Surrounded by Enemies: Troubles and Problems

But notice something about this table. It's smack in front of the enemies. It's in their presence. Yes it is. All of the overwhelming, overflowing blessings in this life are surrounded by our troubles and problems.

Ever had a kid that got distracted from the table? He's just up to get a spoon or a bottle of ketchup, and he gets a little off course as he wanders from what should be a straight and short shot. Pretty soon he's either engulfed in the plot to a corn hole tournament on ESPN or he's navigating Hot Wheels through a traffic jam, complete with sound effects.

It happens, but not just to our children. God has provided great blessings, but we get distracted from the table. Any distractions by the enemies should do one thing, send us straight back to the one who is leading us by the water, restoring our souls. It's a short straight shot.

Instead, we're expending our energy and trying to navigate our own lives through the traffic jams. And most of the time, complete with the sound effects of gloom, despair, and agony with a side of panic. Um, we forgot the table. And we aren't paying attention to the cup running over either.

And More! Anointed Priests

Here's the deal: Not only is the table provided, it's prepared! I love thinking about the care (1 Pet. 5:7) of the one who knows all my problems, all my trials, and all my enemies. And all the while, he is working it out. He's making provisions and preparations for things I don't even know are coming my way yet. When you prepare a table like that, you're in the details. God is in my details. My table is grand. My cup's running over. And my head is anointed.

Oh man, if there's anything I hate, it's a touch of grease in my hair, so I always struggle with understanding the joy of a head anointed with oil, but there *is* joy. The psalmist, most likely David, enjoys a huge blessing not shared by those enemies. He's royalty.

So are we. "But you are a chosen race, a royal priesthood, a holy nation, a people for his own possession, that you may proclaim the excellencies of him who called you out of darkness into his marvelous light" (1 Pet. 2:9). Did you get that? A royal priesthood. Peter was writing to New Testament Christians. We don't go through a priest; we *are* priests. All of us who are his holy nation. Quit staying up in the middle of the night to see a royal wedding or funeral. Go to bed in the luxury of knowing that you are a princess, and in the midst of all of your problems, your Father the King has prepared a royal table for you and filled your cup to overflowing. Considering that, everything's going to be all right.

The Lord is my King and the Lord is my Shepherd. I shall not want. What could I possibly want more? I'm happy.

Perspective

In the spiritual realm ultimately, but also in the physical, we are blessed beyond belief. God has given us precious promises, and has never stopped pouring. Eight chapters into the Bible, he spoke these words that still ring true:

While the earth remains, seedtime and harvest, cold and heat, summer and winter, day and night, shall not cease (Gen. 8:22).

The year, 2021, was one of the most trying years for our fellow Americans that I remember. The only reason I had the time to devote to writing this book was because we were quarantined to home due to a health crisis. This follows tornadoes that hit harder than any I remember, taking away loved ones from some of my dearest friends. We don't know what tomorrow holds. We never do, but I can look at Genesis 8:22 paired with 1 Peter 5:7 and know it's going to be all right. We hurt, but he cares, and he keeps on providing and preparing.

Perspective helps. There's a children's book that's been popular for decades called *Alexander and the Terrible, Horrible, No Good, Very Bad Day* by Judith Viorst. It's one of my favorites, but while the message is "some days are like that, even in Australia," there's a better one. While Alexander keeps repeating through the pages of the book, "It was a terrible, horrible, no good, very bad day," what he should be saying is, "It was an incredibly wonderful, amazing, very good day!"

His cup's running over!

Here's why I say that. When he drops his sweater in the sink while the water is running, this means one thing—running water! How many people in the world have never experienced having running water in their homes? He went to bed with gum in his mouth, and now there's gum in his hair. He has a bed? Even the fact that he has hair to get gum stuck in is a privilege some sick children have lost, at least during cancer treatments. He had hair, a sweater, running water, a bed, and gum— something children in the Philippines would follow you for blocks on end in hopes of getting a piece. And we haven't even gotten past the first page.

Alexander doesn't get a toy in his breakfast cereal, but he got breakfast. He didn't get to sit by the window on the way to school, but he was in a car. He didn't get dessert at lunch, but he had lunch. He didn't get the color of shoes he wanted at the shoe store, but he got brand new shoes! All of his complaints emerged out of blessings if you take a closer look. Need we discuss the bath, dinner, TV, or the night-light? I'm pretty sure what Alexander needs to do is go get a towel. His cup's running over!

It's a children's book written on a second-grade reading level, but it mirrors our own terrible, horrible, no good, very bad days. What we view as negatives are nothing but a lack of appreciation for the positives staring us in the face.

Perspective Applied

Let's never trick a child into thinking that bad days are defined by deviations from our agenda: the wrong color shoes or gum in our hair. And let's never deceive him by teaching him that good days are defined by everything lining up the way we'd like it. It never will, and that's why you see tears and hear wails in big ticket amusement parks because something unforeseen happened to the amusement.

> I was so glad my child had a cavity instead of a tumor.

Mainly, let's let the lesson sink in as adults. I've never much liked dentist days. At all. Especially when I'm the one in the chair. I always dread it for the kids as well. The dentist is very congenial, asking them questions about school and their favorite TV shows as if he doesn't have a drill press on their tongue. Even if they want to cooperate, they can't get a thing out of their mouth that doesn't sound remotely like the word squash-warrior (which was not a top grossing series in my memory). When I see the co-pay, I remember why it is that I further dislike dentist day. We leave with a kid with a numb mouth who suddenly has a craving for corn nuts.

The day I'm about to tell you about, my daughter was the one in the chair. Actually, she was on a recliner adjacent to another little boy. He was telling about an adventure he had just been on with Jack Hannah—a wild safari with lots of exciting creatures.

"Hmm, beats a dentist office," I thought as I looked up from a riveting article in *Orthodontics Quarterly*. But then as the dentist asked more questions of the boy, and the mother made some comments, I began to understand that this was a "Make-a-Wish" adventure. He had been given the trip because he was terminally ill. I was immediately both heartbroken and ashamed. Never had I been so glad to have a child with a cavity instead of a tumor. Never was I so glad to provide a co-pay for a dental visit. I whispered to myself to go get a towel. I was suddenly aware just how much my cup was running over.

No doubt someone reading this has been in the shoes of that gentle mother with her sweet son that day. May we all empathize with compassion, learn contentment, and get perspective.

Goodness and Mercy

As we close this chapter, let's look at how the psalmist closes his chapter. Goodness and mercy are about the best two ideals that could be imagined, and they're following us. All the days of our life. All of them. Like the woman said when I knocked on her door to report that her goat was caught in the fence, "E'erday!" Mercy and goodness are on our heels. As long as the Lord is our Shepherd, thank God we will never get away from those assured realities.

But it gets better because it contrasts that idea, as happy as it is, to another one. We can get through any day here with happiness because, for one thing, mercy and goodness are bringing up the rear, but ultimately, when the days of my life have run out, I will dwell in the house of the Lord forever.

Go get a towel, because that is the ultimate pour-over.

My cup overflows. Surely goodness and mercy shall follow me all the days of my life, and I shall dwell in the house of the Lord forever (Ps. 23:5–6).

# If You're Happy, You Will Know It

1. Recall a time in your life when someone else's pain caused you to reevaluate your perspective.

2. There's a sentence in this chapter that reads, "May we all empathize with compassion, learn contentment, and get perspective." Which one of these three goals do you need to work on the most?

3. Select or make a beautiful card, and write a note to a woman who has lost a child or one who has a terminally ill child, telling her how much you love her, and include a verse of scripture that strengthens you the most.

4. Get your hands on a copy of *Alexander and the Terrible, Horrible, No Good, Very Bad Day*. Make a list of every blessing he has in that book. Circle on your list those that you share too. Now, every day this week, thank God for a different blessing on that list that you usually take for granted.

5. This week, notice children when you are out and about. Focus on finding not just those who want their own way, but those who are grateful, polite, and thankful. How does this change the atmosphere? How do you think it changes the atmosphere when we, as adults, are grateful, polite, and thankful? How do you think it makes God feel?

6. Which is your favorite verse of Psalm 23? Why?

7. In what way are we priests today (1 Pet. 2:9)?

8. When the Lord is our Shepherd, how is it that goodness and mercy follow us? How does God's goodness differ from God's mercy? Give an example of each in your life.

9. Our grand plans for the day get waylaid easily. Recall a time when your day got knocked way off track by something unforeseen. How did you cope with it?

Happy Trails

And speaking of fifth Sunday fellowship meals . . .

I feel sorry for people who don't know. I can't imagine a life lived so empty as to never have known what's at the end of the stairwell, or past the classroom doors to either side of the baptistry, or just across the way in the adjacent building.

It's a thing few dignitaries have seen equaled. It's squash casserole, peach-colored salads, and muddy desserts that ooze Eagle Brand.

Oh, I know that even the "non-churchgoers" have their reunions and big funeral meals, but what a pity to have to wait. We get to eat grand whether anybody dies or not. And we do it a lot. It's almost as if our bodies are on auto-pilot, and as soon as the closing prayer winds up, we start naturally gravitating toward the designated location.

In the 1950s, there were some strong reservations about eating in the building. But on closer observation, it became obvious that 1 Corinthians 11 was a rebuke about abuse of the Lord's supper and not of eating meals together, so we got past it. We got so far past it that we have to stop and remind ourselves that we can actually make other uses of the building too, in addition to eating. Skeptics may accuse us of only being in it for the loaves and fishes, but they are dreadfully wrong. There is Mexican cornbread too.

General Motors may be in financial straits, the stock market may be plummeting, but as long as we're around, the cream of mushroom soup company is in good shape.

There are unspoken rules, but they are rigid. Each congregation has her own, which can make it embarrassing if you're a visitor and, after being urged to go first in line, you choose the spot to sit that has been the men's table for the past fifty years.

It takes a lifetime of experience to master the sport of fellowship meals. As a child, I ignorantly wanted to be first in line. I also knew there was nothing that would get me a quicker "Alabama hickory whippin'" than to try it, so I spent the first few minutes hiding under the stairs reaching through the open spaces and grabbing boys' shoes as they stumbled toward the feast. Then I casually blended into the line mid-way.

As an adult, I know my mother was just trying to look out for me. It's way better to get at the end of the line. You get to go down both sides with nobody looking at how much you're getting, and no guilt of wondering if there will be enough for those behind you. I've learned more tricks of the trade as I've traveled.

This next tip comes from a mountain town in Arkansas: Eat the dessert while everyone else is getting the main course. You can do it under the guise of helping out in the kitchen. In West Tennessee I learned to bring a heavy-duty plate from home and you don't have to worry about it folding up and giving way under pressure.

For all the joy of fellowship meals, they do have a flipside. It's pretty hard to get through four verses of "All things are ready, come to the feast" with your heart in the right place when the aroma of turnip greens and sweet potatoes are drifting in from the foyer. And we face uncomfortable dilemmas such as, after all these years of fried chicken being the central course, is it really scriptural to grill? And when five people volunteer to pick up the fish for the widow after worship, does she know it's because they take their cut on the way back? And when my mother griped for two miles on the way to church because she bet her sister would only bring one bowl of peas, can we excuse her because she gave us such a great "Martha" illustration? Further problems ensue when our desserts usually outnumber our other courses two to one, and we get so caught up in the "covered dish" part that we've forgotten the "covered drink," forcing us on more than one occasion, I promise, to run next door to the nursing home and borrow a Sprite.

But it's here that I learned the principle of joy over circumstances. I remember years ago the radio blaring out a song about an all-day singing and dinner on the ground. I didn't know what it meant, but I assumed it had to do with those times my mother was so concerned with having enough that she had us march in with two or three bowls each. Inevitably, there would be a pile of macaroni and cheese or au gratin potatoes in the parking lot. Mark it down; it was whatever she spent the most time preparing. Regrettably, it was dinner on the ground. But there were no tears as we skipped on into Bible class postponing the clean-up until a more convenient season. My mother burned a cake one Sunday morning, and I asked her what I could do to help her. "Ice it and take it," came the answer. It has become the coping catchphrase in my home.

The fun goes on. The "fellowship meal" is not a place for those who treasure quiet. We're not concerned with ambiance as we squeeze down cinder-block halls. Our immediate food reviews do not consist of counting how many lavish tiers exist or an analysis of the cut of meat in a dish we cannot pronounce, but there is an untamed hubbub over which we can discern an occasional "Who made this?" and "That is mighty fittin'."

It may cause us to take a second look at gluttony, but it gives us fiber that we can't count in grams. When everything else is trying to pull us apart, it truly pulls us together. We push ourselves back from the table to another week of chaos. Bring it on.

We'll ice it and take it.

Originally published in Christian Woman *magazine, 2010.*

4

IF MAMA AIN'T HAPPY,
She's Got Too Many Columns

Sing the Blues Or Embrace the Trials

The pros and the cons. The plus signs and minus signs. The good and the bad. Archie Campbell was famous way too many years ago to remember his "that's good; that's bad" comedy routine. We have our own version of that comedy routine most days. I remember one day in particular when we were coming back from the Lads to Leaders convention, and our congregation had allowed my husband, the preacher, to take the entire Sunday off. That's good. Well, it was, but when we were trying to find a place to stop for worship that night, we were running behind. That's bad. We pulled into the parking lot on two wheels just in time. That's good. Not really, because my husband didn't see the speed bump, and when he hit it, I was putting on my make-up, and my loose powder went everywhere. That's bad. No, it's okay because I had a pillow on my lap, and most of it went there instead of on my outfit. That's good. Yes, but when I got out of the car, I needed to get all that powder off the pillow so I began beating it on the side of the car. That's bad. Now we kind of looked like Pigpen in the Charlie Brown comic strip with a cloud of dust around us, but it did a fair job of cleaning the pillow. That's good.

Yes, so we started heading for the church building, and one of my kids said, "You can't go in there like that; you've got socks on with your sandals." That's bad. Well, I had been cold in the car, and had put the socks on, and since I have never been much of a fashion model anyway, I let the kid know quickly that I didn't care, and proceeded toward the door. That's good. It is, except she loudly protested, "But there's a hole in your sock!" That's bad.

One column: the joy column.

Yep, so I decided to take off the socks to keep from embarrassing my children. That's good. Except it's not easy to do when you're in a gravel church parking lot, so I held myself up with one hand on the kid and the other on the car. That's bad. Well, it wasn't easy, especially when one of the other kids was extremely concerned with being on time. That's good. I guess it is good, but he was hurrying me. That's bad. Yes, and so I said, "I'm trying!" That's good. It would be if I hadn't followed it with "I didn't know I was going to have to do *a strip show in the parking lot!*" That's bad. Well, my husband headed straight back for me, I thought, to help me. That's good. And he said, "Celine, can you keep it down? We have a greeter out here to welcome us." That's bad.

My apologies to anyone who witnessed any of this, but the point is, we do tend to categorize things as either good or bad. We place the good things in the happy column. That's joy. We place the bad things in the negative column. That's not joy. James tells us in James 1 we've got too many columns.

One Column

James gets straight to the point at the very beginning of the letter. Verse 1 is basically, "Hey, how's everybody doing?" and verse 2 and following is full-on encouragement for hard days.

> *Count it all joy, my brothers, when you meet trials of various kinds, for you know that the testing of your faith produces steadfastness. And let steadfastness have its full effect, that you may be perfect and complete, lacking in nothing (James 1:2–4).*

Count it all joy. One column. The joy column. It all goes there. When it comes to life, don't do the math wrong, because it's especially easy to do the math wrong when you stick numbers in the wrong column.

He says even to count it all joy when we fall into trials. Is he sure? I mean, in some trials we might see some benefit. I'm not sure he understands the difficulties a few of us are going through here. What kind of trials are you talking about, James?

Trials of various kinds. The whole range. The NKJV says "various" and the KJV says "divers." Our trials are diverse, but I think James is reiterating that it's all of them.

Look at the next three words, "for you know." We know something that's key to this understanding. We know something that the world doesn't know. "For you know that the testing of your faith works steadfastness." Steadfastness means holding on tight. It's like the song we often sing from Lamentations 3:22: "The Steadfast Love of the Lord Never Ceases." The holding-on-tight love of the Lord gives us beautiful imagery. We develop that holding-on-tight quality through these trials. They give us perseverance, endurance, and patience—three words that appear in various translations of this verse. I grew up memorizing it as patience.

However, I don't think our current use of the word *patience* does the verse justice. We use patience for those times when we wait in the line for our kid to sit in Santa Claus's lap, and we suddenly know where the phrase "slow as Christmas" originated. Or we use it on a rainy day when we play Uno with a second grader one more time than there are cards in the deck. Or when we sit through a sixth-grade band concert waiting for our nephew's solo, which turns out to be three notes if you count the long one as two.

Patience has come to mean waiting without losing it, and that is a big part of it (Ps. 27:14). This trying of our faith gives patience a workout. Do you see that word *work* in James 1:4? It works us, and workouts are hard on us but beneficial. It didn't take Kelly Clarkson to tell us what doesn't kill you makes you stronger. What's stronger than patience is patience that's been working out, and we call that endurance, perseverance, steadfastness. It's holding on, going the long haul no matter what. We know that.

What Else Do We Know?

We get the same kind of encouragement about getting through the worst because of the best in Romans 8, and probably our favorite, or at least most quoted, verse out of the whole chapter is verse 28. It starts with the same idea, "And we know." "And we know that for those who love God all things work together for good, for those who are called according to his purpose."

If we know it, we've got to both let it work us out and let him work it out. "And let steadfastness have its full effect," James 1:4 says. That little bitty word *let* presents a great big challenge. This is the hardest part. We've got to let it happen. We meet adversity kicking and screaming. We want to take a shortcut or a bypass or a ditch if we can hide in it, but we find sometimes there is just no other way, and so we "let" steadfastness have its full effect.

And what happens next? The good part. Every time these tests tried to loosen your grip, you tightened it, and suddenly the results are in. "That you may be perfect and complete, lacking in nothing." The results are perfect, not that you are sinless but you're not senseless either. You're whole; you're well; you're complete. It's like the Great Physician has looked at the heart scan after all the grueling treatments, and said, "Perfect."

The Holy Spirit draws a better word here:

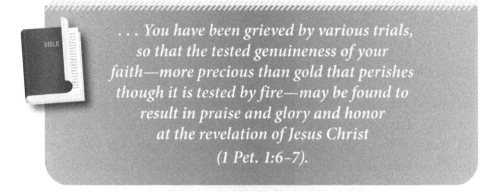

. . . You have been grieved by various trials, so that the tested genuineness of your faith—more precious than gold that perishes though it is tested by fire—may be found to result in praise and glory and honor at the revelation of Jesus Christ
(1 Pet. 1:6–7).

Similar to James's language, Peter says, "grieved by various trials." Where's the happy part in that? It gets worse before it gets better as he compares these tests to gold as it is put through fire in the purification process. We feel like that sometimes, but what can be more valuable than the gold produced? A soul! Your soul. My soul. Peter is quick to point out that gold is just a perishable in the whole scheme of things. But at that time of the revelation of Jesus Christ, our inheritance has only begun; it's eternal. Praise! Glory! Honor!

The Joy Column

If Mama ain't happy, she's trying to wriggle out of that "trials" column and get into that happy one over there. It's all the same one for the Christian. Take a second look at this passage in 1 Peter 1. Right *before* the trials and gold-in-the-fire part, which he says is just for a little while, he emphasizes the heaven part saying, "In this you rejoice" (v. 6). It's the same concept Jesus kept bringing up on that mountainside, remember? Right *after* the trials and gold-in-the-fire part, Peter talks about "joy that is inexpressible" (v. 8). It's happiness beyond what we can put into words.

I'm not saying it's not hard. Job's period of testing was hard. Paul's trials appear to me to have been exceedingly hard, though his letters radiate contentment and joy. I am thinking of a friend whose storms have just been exceptionally hard beyond what most people encounter in a lifetime. But there is one, and only one, whose hardship far surpassed anything we could, in our most painful breath, begin to comprehend.

Your Suffering Perspective

Because all our hope lies in the reality of the cross, we embrace it in everything from our songs to our jewelry. It's easy, in our celebration of the salvation emerging from it, to forget the merciless cruelty and agony within it. It wasn't enough that Christ emptied himself of the glory of deity and died on our behalf, but the event was made even more significant because it took the form of the very apex of suffering. In thorns, it crowned all other deaths. With nails, he was pierced. In anguish, he struggled for a breath, his body already drenched in blood from a beating with the worst of Roman implements. No wonder after Philippians 2:8 says, "He humbled himself by becoming obedient to the point of death," it emphasizes, "even death on a cross."

At times we measure our strength by the ability to welcome oncoming pain, but the strongest one who ever lived had such dread of the looming cross, that "being in agony he prayed more earnestly; and his sweat became like great drops of blood falling down to the ground" (Luke 22:44). Which one of us can say our trials have ever reached that level?

The Joy Set before Him

When we realize this, what I'm about to tell you is even more remarkable, if not unfathomable. Jesus counted it as joy. Hebrews 12:2 tells us that he endured it, even though he despised the shame of it, for the joy that was set before him. I believe, as the passage tells us, that the joy involved his returning to the Father. But I also believe that the joy involved our returning to the Father. There was no other reason for the cross to happen. There was no other reason for him to endure the severity and shame, except that it afforded me salvation.

It was the only means by which I could be reconciled to God.

It is the ultimate joy of the Lord. And now, because it happened—Praise God, because it happened—it is our ultimate joy.

James ends the counting lesson in James 1 by saying that we will be "lacking in nothing" (v. 4). What a conclusion! When we see the joy through the lens of the cross, it is a joy that screams, what else could we want? Which takes us right back to the lesson learned in the previous chapter of this book: "The Lord is my shepherd; I shall not want."

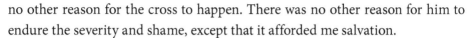

> *Looking to Jesus, the founder and perfecter of our faith, who for the joy that was set before him endured the cross, despising the shame, and is seated at the right hand of the throne of God (Heb. 12:2).*

 If You're Happy, You Will Know It

1. Add the following numbers: 31, 94, 52, 02, and 20. Write down your total. Now add these: 31, 94, 25, 20, and 20. Write that sum. Now notice that all of the digits in both addition problems were the same, but some, in fact only a couple of times, were rearranged to a different column. In math class, we say, the values are in the wrong place. What do we say in the bigger classroom? Do misplaced values affect the sum of who we are? How? And what if it's only in a couple of areas?

2. James identifies himself in James 1:1 as a servant of Christ when he could have identified himself as the brother of Christ. How does that shed light on his views in the next few verses?

3. Do you agree that the same trials can either tighten your grip or loosen it? How and why?

4. Soon after James says we will be "lacking in nothing," he says, "If any of you lacks wisdom." How can it be that if we lack nothing, we can lack wisdom? Is this wisdom after the fact, or wisdom needed during the trial? Which makes more sense in the context?

5. Besides the first verse of Psalm 23 and the last part of James 1:4, what other parallels do you see between these two passages?

Happy Trails

And speaking of socks . . .

It is better to give than to receive, especially when you're receiving a very large box which, upon opening, strikes in you the realization that a stove backsplash has the exact same measurements of a flat screen TV. Some of us are pretty good at dropping hints about as subtle as an anvil on a bare toe. And some of us are about as good at picking up on those as an eleven-year-old boy is at picking up socks.

Speaking of socks, it's hard to get through a Christmas without them. Yet I guess I could say I've never seen a kid running laps around the tree yelling, "Socks, socks!" and posting pictures for all his friends to envy. And yet we still give it a whirl. Every Christmas. It's kind of like cranberry sauce. Nobody wants it, but it's just there.

My husband's grandmother cuts to the chase when it comes to socks on Christmas. No more digging for a pocket knife to cut away the curly ribbon while everyone is watching, and then posing with the socks held up to your smiling face as if this was at the very top of your wish list. She brings out the sock tub as a commercial break in the festivities. It's obvious she has bought out the entire hosiery department at Sears, and for fear that the last person will get a pair of the dull grey thin dress ones, everyone scrambles like the Hope diamond has been dropped in the bottom of the tub.

I guess the fact that it's the one thing people will not bother to take back drives the price up on these things at the retailers to the degree that if they put a half-inch horse on the side, they can extract sixteen dollars from a tired shopper the weekend before Christmas.

I know of a lady—true story—who was entrusted with the responsibility to help an older man shop for his wife. After she made the purchase for him (high end socks), she finished the day with some shopping for herself (high end dress). The problem is she didn't look in the bag closely enough, or at all, before handing the man the sock purchase for his wife. You guessed it—the wife was elated with such an expensive dress, and was amazed her husband would have been so thoughtful. He couldn't believe he got this much bang for his twelve bucks. It was better than a sitcom.

I wouldn't want you to think all our gift-giving revolves around socks. Dollar Tree has other items too. When we were growing up, we opened our hearts and Mickey Mouse wallets to invest in such things. My sister hovered over household happenings year-round, but she stepped up security during the holidays. If you were caught shaking a gift, you became aware that while the rest of the church was caught up in wondering what the unpardonable sin is, you were pretty sure you had just discovered it. No hints, no touching, no reading name tags under the tree were allowed.

We thought we were reliving D-Day when the unthinkable happened, and a family member uttered what should have never crossed human lips—the first syllable of a package's contents, namely "mi." Loud wailing ensued as my sister slammed her head on the table, crying, "Mirror, mirror, you got me a mirror, and you told me. How could you?" It was probably a ten-cent gift, but her disappointment at spoiling her Christmas morning surprise was reminiscent of David's "Absalom, Absalom" eulogy. I didn't dare say out loud what I was thinking, which was, "I think you could use that mirror right now."

We grew up, and while it might not have seemed possible at the time, we got over it. Now we don't reveal what's in the packages because, quite frankly, we can't remember. I was glad it was just our immediate family this year when I said, "Okay, I think this is the gift. Everyone watch. This is great." I had made a funny T-shirt for a family member, but I forgot I had also been bra shopping.

Not only do we forget what's in the packages, but pretty soon we forget who got what. This is detrimental to re-gifting because the same sister who was once absorbed with co-authoring the congressional Top-Secret Gift Giving Act is now so unattached to the package contents that she has been known to gift-wrap arbitrary items lying around and give them directly back to the original giver.

And so it's time to face the dilemma again. Yeah, it's more blessed to give than to receive, but what to give? You can wrap a beehive in a huge exciting box for a five-year-old. You can wrap up a twenty-dollar gift card knowing full well you could save a step because the thing the person wants most with the gift card is twenty dollars. You can roll four white-wall tires in through the kitchen door and make the cut for the next Jeff Foxworthy book. Our friends and family have tried all of these, and they have all led to one conclusion.

Socks are safest.

Originally published in Christian Woman *magazine, November/December 2015.*

5

IF MAMA AIN'T HAPPY,

There's More Than a Pad on That Shoulder

Fester or Forgive

You can't make this stuff up. I was en route to New Zealand, and had made it as far as Houston. We loaded onto the plane at 10:00 PM for the long, long flight, but there was a delay before we left the ground. They needed to replace a wiper blade on the jet, but were having difficulty finding the part. We sat there another good forty-five minutes before they announced that the part was found, but they couldn't contact the technician responsible for replacing it. When this was finally resolved, they reported that there was another mechanical failure of some kind, and the next thing I knew, we were sitting on the floor of an empty terminal waiting for the next news. By 3:00 AM I was in line to be assigned a hotel room. By 5:00 AM I was in it for my two hours of beauty rest.

Within twelve hours, after I had jumped the most ridiculous hurdles only to get to several more dead ends, I was rushed to a totally different airline clutching a hand-scribbled itinerary, and was told I was going to Los Angeles and from there to Australia (I know), but there was no time to check my bags. I would have to carry them all over the Los Angeles airport. Raise your hand if you've ever been to the Los Angeles airport. It makes the Atlanta airport look like a trip to the fridge and back. You run for miles to catch your plane, which might work if your bags had been checked, but I was basically the front end of a U-Haul pushing a wheelbarrow and balancing a luggage rack on my head.

I was in the publishing stages of a book, and the publisher had given me a three-ring bound copy to look over in the luxury of some of my more convenient layovers (laugh track here), so I had been carrying it under one arm or balancing it on top of a roller bag. There are at least sixty-eight nice people in Los Angeles, because on the sixty-eighth time I dropped it and someone picked it up for me, I had a realization. I came to myself. It occurred to me that it was replaceable, that I could dispose of it, and my life would become so much easier. All of this time, I had been holding on to something that was unnecessary, it was hindering all of my other progress, and when I let go of it for good, and didn't pick it up again, I experienced a tremendous freedom.

Transgression Luggage

That's how it is with the unwillingness to forgive. We carry something around with us that is really unnecessary. We can't undo the fact that the transgression or offense happened and we were hurt by it, and so we choose to keep being hindered by it, to keep lugging it around, when really, if we'd just let go of it once and for all, we would experience full freedom.

Jesus had a lot to say about forgiveness. The entire Bible never veers far from the topic really because man's transgression comes early, and God's great plan for forgiveness is the thread that brings us all the way to the cross establishing a pathway of entry into heaven. Without forgiveness, all is lost.

In Matthew 18, Peter brought the subject up and asked how many times he was expected to forgive his brother. He wondered if seven times would be about right. The problem with Peter's question was that he wasn't really focusing on when he should forgive, but on when he could stop forgiving.

We need to check our focus. Sometimes I will speak on the subject of forgiveness or I will be in an audience where it has been addressed, and a discussion will inevitably ensue afterwards in which questions begin with the words "What if … ?" or "Do we really have to … ?" or "How can we … ?" Often I notice that our very questions, like Peter's, are far more wrapped up in what allowances we have not to forgive, than in the joy of true forgiveness.

We all know Jesus' answer to Peter:

> *I do not say to you seven times,*
> *but seventy-seven times*
> *(Matt. 18:22).*

I think we get the meaning. We just should not have a cap on forgiveness. Aren't we glad God doesn't?

Exaggerated Debt

Jesus jumps right to that point in the very next verse as he begins a parable we've all heard. There was a king who, on a certain day, decided to settle accounts with his servants. Among them was a man who owed ten thousand talents. That's huge. One talent was equal to fifteen years' wages. I'm pretty sure that if I owed someone the average of fifteen years' wages, I would never be able to repay that debt. But this isn't just one talent. This isn't just thirty or forty talents. This is ten thousand talents. If you start doing the math here, this servant didn't owe millions, in our currency, but billions.

Why does Jesus use a number so very large? Remember, the first servant represents each one of us. The debt of sin is so huge that there is no way we are able to repay it. Without forgiveness, all is lost.

The picture gets more pitiful as the parable continues. The punishment is so severe that it's unbearable. Since the servant is unable to pay, the king demands that he, his wife, and children be sold on the auction block, along with every-thing he has. At that, the servant hits his knees begging for more time. It's what I would have done. I have four children, and if at any time something this horrific stared any one of them in the face, I would beg, plead, blockade them with my own body, and cry out for mercy, "Give me more time!" There's not enough time in the world to pay a debt like that. For me. Or for that servant that day.

And so the king had compassion. Wonderful, celebratory compassion. He did not give him more time; he did not lessen the amount; he did not reduce the sentence or ease the severity of the punishment; he forgave the debt. Fully.

Let it sink in. My own situation was so desperate that a lesser sentence was impossible. My verdict was guilty, and my outlook beyond bleak. The only hope was in a compassionate King. Hallelujah, he forgave the debt! Paid in full on the cross of Calvary. Who wouldn't accept that pardon?

In the midst of dire cries of the realization that all is undone, "Brothers, what shall we do?" (Acts 2:37), Peter assured the crowd on Pentecost of the par-don: "Repent and be baptized every one of you in the name of Jesus Christ for the forgiveness of your sins, and you will receive the gift of the Holy Spirit." I'll take it. Up from the ground, from wailing to euphoria. If Mama ain't happy, does she know the compassionate King?

Paul said it best:

> *Thanks be to God for his inexpressible gift!*
> *(2 Cor. 9:15).*

"Paltry" in Perspective

Oh, that the story had ended there for the servant. Plot twist. The forgiven ser-vant walked free, and walked straight to the one who owed him a lesser debt, a hundred denarii. I don't know a lot about Roman currency, but it seems it was possibly substantial—maybe a couple of thousand dollars, enough to sting a little.

After all, one denarius was a whole day's wages in Matthew 20:2. In the parable of the "good Samaritan," two denarii would cover several days lodging and care (Luke 10:35). Take the bill for what they call on game shows a four-day/three-night stay (which always confused me) in a luxurious hotel, multiply it by fifty, and we're getting a picture of the value of a hundred denarii. In the episode of Jesus feeding five-thousand-plus people, Phillip said that even two hundred denarii wouldn't be enough to buy food for a crowd that size (John 6:7), as if two hundred denarii was a honking big amount. In John 12, Judas estimates that the perfume the woman brought Jesus was so expensive that it could have been sold for three hundred denarii. I'm beginning to believe that when you get three digits in front of the word denarii, you're in the money!

The hurt is paltry compared to my sin debt.

How does that fit in this parable? What am I saying here? Haven't we always thought that the lesser amount was paltry, and the first servant should have immediately shrugged it off.

Well, that loses some of the application for me. Of course, it's easy to shrug off something that's shruggable. But what we struggle with are those things that are downright painful. We're just not willing to forgive because the hurt cuts too deep.

Wait, did we just align ourselves with the merciless servant? Match. Same.

But Jesus puts these two events in the same parable for a reason. Suddenly, that thing that we steam over, that makes us sick to the stomach, really is—no matter what it is—paltry. It's paltry compared to the sin debt I could not pay if I had a hundred lives to pay it. It's forgiven. Now, it's my move.

Somewhere between Resentment and Disdain

The forgiven servant grabbed the other man, began choking him, and said, "Pay what you owe" (Matt. 18:28). The man who owed the smaller amount now hit his knees and began to plead for more time. Deja vu. Except this time, the once-forgiven servant had no compassion but put him in prison until he could pay the debt.

Are we feeling a tinge of guilt about now? I wonder if Peter shuffled his feet a little bit, fidgeted in his sandals, and put his hands in the pockets of that first century garb. If it didn't hit home for Peter, it does for me. Prison. After we've been completely free from the sin debt, we want to put our brother or sister in a holding place until we're sure. We'll put them somewhere between resentment and disdain, a place cut off from us until we see enough good deeds or change to make up for what they did.

I have sinned against the Lord.

—David

But the king was told about the situation. In all of this parable, the parallels are obvious. This is the only detail that really differs from our own reality. Our King doesn't have to be told. He knows exactly what we've done and how we feel toward our brother or sister the second the thought comes into our head.

How to Erase Your Pardon

I hate to carry you through to the horrible end, but I hate not to, because parables serve as warnings. The tragedy in the fiction can prevent the tragedy in the reality: the first servant, forgiven such a tremendous debt, had erased his own pardon through his unwillingness to forgive another. "His master delivered him to the jailers, until he could pay his debt" (Matt. 18:34). Instead of "jailers," the KJV reads "tormentors," and the NKJV "torturers."

Who's telling the parable? The one with all authority (Matt. 28:18). If the one with all authority talks about the place of eternal punishment as a place of weeping and gnashing of teeth over and over again in the New Testament (Luke 13:28; Matt. 8:12; et al.), I believe he knows what he's talking about. Torture is not a stretch.

The parable has drawn the audience in, in both the first century and the twenty-first, but the culmination of its truth is in verse 35 (Matt. 18), and truly in three words of it.

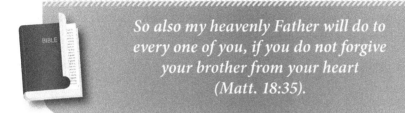

> *So also my heavenly Father will do to every one of you, if you do not forgive your brother from your heart (Matt. 18:35).*

There are the three words: *from your heart.* It's not enough to express the words; it's not enough to smile from a distance while you seethe on the inside. It has to be a complete job, all the way from the heart.

"Unforgiving" Words

We have to reach that point. I sat across the table from a woman in a Tex-Mex restaurant several years ago. I hardly knew her that day; I have since come to love her. She was telling me the recent events that had happened to those in her family. There was a betrayal; there were some actions that weren't even legal, much less within God's will; there was embarrassment and heartbreak, and all of this came from someone who had been deeply trusted. After sin's miserable, ugly, and vile outpouring of pain, the offender repented. And as my friend was telling me these things, I just let her get it all out. She finally said, "And when someone repents after being caught, you wonder if they've really repented, or if it's just because they were caught." As soon as she said that out loud, she heard herself. Thank God she heard herself. Her eyes widened. Her expression changed. She looked straight at me and repented herself. She said, "that's wrong," and her tears backed up her resolve.

Hear yourself. Hear yourself if you have unforgiving words, and repent before you get to the part about "so also my heavenly Father will do to every one of you if . . . !"

And by the way, even if someone does repent because they get caught, it still counts! If it is true and sincere repentance, we ought to rejoice no matter how it comes about. David was as caught as a skunk in a pine box in 2 Samuel 12. When caught, he said, "I have sinned against the Lord," and the very next sentence in the conversation is, "The Lord also has put away your sin." God is the quickest Forgiver of all! How is it that we're so slow?

> *David said to Nathan, "I have sinned against the Lord." And Nathan said to David, "The Lord also has put away your sin; you shall not die"*
> *(2 Sam. 12:13).*

Linking "Forgive" with "Forgiven"

Jesus repeatedly links our forgiven status with our willingness to forgive others. We don't like to link those. I believe one of the finest glimpses we're given into the apostles' hearts happens in Luke 11. Whereas their questions were prone to reflect self-ambition, if not downright envy, this time the request revealed a Godward desire. It was simply, "Lord, teach us to pray." May we all lay aside self-ambition and simply ask the same.

Jesus' answer on this occasion has been treasured for centuries. We have committed the answer to memory in its entirety. In my elementary school, a public government-funded school, it was repeated every morning over the intercom system. What could possibly be a better way to start a day? And so, whether because of its sheer familiarity, beautiful words, or treasured sentiment, we hear portions of it often in our assembly's public prayers. It's not unusual for those leading to begin with "Our Father in Heaven, hallowed be your name." Neither is it unusual to hear, "Give us this day our daily bread." It certainly is repeated in at least ninety-nine percent of the prayers we offer, "Forgive us our sins," but it breaks up right after that. You almost never hear the next phrase, "for we ourselves forgive everyone who is indebted to us" (Luke 11:1–4).

Why? Jesus teaches the same prayer in Matthew 6, and this version says, "and forgive us our debts, *as* we also have forgiven our debtors" (v. 12). Whether we say "as" or "for," it indicates there is a relationship between the fullness of God's forgiving us and the degree of fullness with which we forgive others. We just don't like to say that out loud because it's frightening to ask for the same kind of forgiveness from God that we give to someone who's hurt us.

Don't Rob Yourself!

If God forgave us the way we forgive others, we know it sometimes would fall short. Sometimes it would be "forgiveness," but not yet—not until you've suffered awhile and I've steamed over it first. It would sometimes be a resolve to forgive but never forget. We would forgive with the contingency of it being the last time we will, especially if it's already the seventh. The truth is, we don't want God to forgive us like that. We love to think of God's erasing our sins (Acts 22:16), remembering them no more (Heb. 8:12), and removing them completely from sight, mind, and reach (Ps. 103:12).

Can we really forgive as we are forgiven? We must! As if forgiveness really lies in our hands. It does to the degree that we're commanded to do it. But how presumptuous of us to think that by holding out on forgiveness, we are somehow determining an outcome.

Forgiveness is God's alone; he just enables us the joy of it for our own benefit and for healing. He's the real one who is sinned against. He's the one who paid the price; he's the one who gave the ultimate sacrifice. And yet he allows us the privilege to also forgive as he forgives. Don't rob yourself of that happiness.

Why have I spent so much time on the topic of forgiveness? This is supposed to be a book on happiness. If we did it right, this really ought to be the first chapter. If we harbor resentment and bitterness, happiness is an unattainable goal. It just is. A person simply cannot be happy when she chooses not to forgive. Happiness is a choice, remember? When we choose to let go of the past and embrace the offender, we can then see clearly to pursue the true happiness addressed in the other chapters. But if not, throw it all away. God wants so badly to forgive you. So much. So much that he sacrificed his Son for it. But you can't reach that forgiveness if there's something in the way.

Joseph's Shoulders: No Chips

The Joseph of Genesis, dreamer of dreams, was also the victim of victims. He was on the receiving end of thoughtlessness, abuse, reckless endangerment, lies, and cruelty. And yet he kept getting back up each time he was kicked down. He kept his chin up until it sprouted a postiche. His brothers didn't like him and landed him in a pit, but everywhere he went after that, despite his position as a slave or a prisoner, he was well-favored. He was liked to the degree he was promoted to the top. People who are unhappy all the time are not well-favored.

He kept getting back up.

He could have held so many grudges. He could have had a whole bag of chips on his shoulder. He chose happiness instead, to the degree he was walking through the prison asking other people, "Why are your faces downcast today?" (Gen. 40:7).

Ultimately, in God's providence, Joseph came face to face with the ones who had mistreated him the most. And now he was in a position of power. He had the political authority to get even. Those brothers who had hated him and would have killed him had lived with a guilty conscience for twenty-two years. It was unbelievable to them that they now stood in his presence, in fear of him, but Joseph said to them, "And now do not be distressed or angry with yourselves because you sold me here, for God sent me before you to preserve life" (Gen. 45:5). Add to this response that he kissed them all and wept (v. 15), and you have the most beautiful display of forgiveness, aside from that of our Savior, in all of scripture, and perhaps in all of history.

Build Walls or Bridges?

When things could get ugly, make them beautiful instead. I always say the two most beautiful things in life are repentance and forgiveness. I have a friend who reminds me of Joseph in the magnitude of her forgiveness. She is so wise and joyful that I have mentioned her in another of my books, but not by name.

Her husband decided he wanted more freedom, wanted to experience the pleasures of sin, but quickly learned just as scriptures tell us, that these pleasures are a high-speed chase leading to inevitable disaster. He left my friend, and after a flurry of fun and wealth and everything worldly, he woke up one day in a homeless shelter, having had everything snatched from him that Satan once dangled in front of him. Sin's wages had arrived, but what we call the regular kind of wages weren't anywhere tangible. He worked in exchange for a place to pillow his head.

But then cancer came calling. The shelter couldn't support this kind of need, and so he had nowhere to go, and he wouldn't have been in the shape to get there if he did. He was the prodigal son in tattered blue jeans, and with an oncology report. That's when my friend did what she does so well; she cared about a person. Her forgiveness opened her home back up to the man who had once left it. He was given a bed and nutrition and medical care, and lots of prayers ascended for his soul.

Slowly, as he witnessed that kind of forgiveness, the layers that had encrusted his heart began to peel away, and bitterness turned to resolve which turned to enthusiasm. He was restored to the Lord, rejoiced in new hope, and only grieved the fact that he was physically incapable to work more in the kingdom.

Sin's wages had arrived.

I wish sin's story ended as well every time. Much of it is up to us, and our willingness to forgive. We don't know what opportunities we will be given. Joseph no more expected to see his brothers again than they did to see him. My friend could not have forecasted such a drastic change in circumstances. In each case, the perpetrator's crimes had brought them full-circle, back to the one they offended. It may happen to you or me. We will choose our response. Forgiveness builds bridges. Unforgiveness builds walls.

Check Your Shoulders

Isn't it ironic that unforgiveness attempts to punish the offender, but destroys instead the one who will not forgive? There is not a single thing I can change, by being unforgiving, about the condition of another person's soul. But when I refuse to forgive, I have changed the status of my own soul.

What's that on your shoulder? In the nineties, we all tried to be triangles, as we had huge geometric shapes protruding from our shoulders. It was the era when shoulder pads took on a life of their own. We could knock things off of shelves when we walked through a room and not feel a thing. Then an issue of *Let-Us-Tell-You-What-to-Wear Quarterly* came out, and that was it. No more shoulder pads. And just like that, our shoulders looked like shoulders again.

What are you shouldering? Are you destroying a lot of things in your path because of what's on your shoulder? Is it a chip or a whole potato? The damage we can do is primarily to our own heart, but people are watching. Children are growing and learning, and if you're willing to cause damage there, you better start taking swim lessons with a millstone around your neck (Matt. 18:6).

If Mama ain't happy, she may be carrying more than a shoulder pad. We don't need a fashion magazine to tell us it's time to get rid of it. There's another publication that's thousands of years old that makes it quite clear. "So also my heavenly Father will do to every one of you, if you do not forgive your brother from your heart" (Matt. 18:35). Let that sink in, and just like that, our shoulders can look like shoulders again.

Let all bitterness and wrath and anger and clamor and slander be put away from you, along with malice. Be kind to one another, tenderhearted, forgiving one another, as God in Christ forgave you (Eph. 4:31–32).

 # If You're Happy, You Will Know It

1. Read Matthew 18:35. How significant are the words "from your heart"? Is there a forgiveness that is not from the heart?

2. In Jesus' parable in Matthew 18, we find a servant begging and pleading with the king. Think of a time where you have begged and pleaded with your King. Did it involve your children? What would you have given, at that point, to have your request granted?

3. What are the dangers of throwing someone in prison until they can pay their debt? In other words, when we decide to postpone forgiveness until we have seen enough penitence, what are the dangers? There may be several you could list.

4. What do you find to be the most disturbing part of this parable in Matthew 18, or the most uncomfortable?

5. Do the math. If a talent is a year's salary, how much would the first servant owe in today's current market?

6. To put it in perspective in biblical times, read 1 Kings 10:14. How much more or less is this debt in Matthew 18, than the yearly income of King Solomon? How does this help us appreciate our condition without Christ's compassion?

7. Make a list of everyone and everything in this parable in Matthew 18 on the left side of your page. On the right side, put what that person or thing represents in your own life.

Happy Trails

And speaking of flights and airports . . .

"We are now inviting all passengers for flight 4221 to Cincinnati in zones one, two, and three to board the plane." That's about the moment that sheer terror wakes within me. I'm not particularly scared of being 25,000 feet above sea level, even when there is no sea. It's not that I'm putting my life into the hands of a pilot who, I promise, could not make it down the down escalator without a system failure. I can't make stuff like that up. I watched as the pilot got his suitcase jammed in the steps, and they had to shut the thing off as the co-pilot helped him pull his bag loose. It was a great laugh for them; a little unsettling for the rest of us.

But no, that's not the real reason that panic sets in. I confess I have a fear of boarding the wrong jet. I sometimes go in the wrong restroom; I take the wrong exit ramp; and I have sat in the wrong McDonald's for forty-five minutes waiting on the person I was supposed to have breakfast with. So I keep checking those numbers, and I tell myself that they won't let me on if I have the wrong boarding pass. But still, there is that luggage jammed in the escalator thing, and my confidence is a little shaky.

It's not just this, but recently my flight was delayed because the battery was dead. What?! The technician had left the emergency lights on all night, and they're telling me this? Wouldn't you think they would just make something up that was a little more reassuring? The airline staff is beginning to remind me of myself. Next they'll tell me that the air traffic controller accidentally left his glasses in the bathroom, and can't see a thing. I suddenly think I have a great future in this career.

Oh well, in the middle of a conversation with the helpful announcer-person about how many of my flights today will be missed because of this delay, and which flights to take instead, she suddenly says, "Never mind. Even though we told you it would take thirty minutes to charge the battery, we think fifteen is good. Everyone board immediately. Hurry!"

Now that any inner security I had is completely shattered, I check the numbers one more time, and then terror turns to dread. I know that the hardest part of the entire trip, the most treacherous and uncertain, is the part where you walk down the aisle to find your seat. This is a sideways walk and you suck it in with all your might, and put your purse single file in front of you, also sideways, and still somehow manage to hit someone on the side of the head with your elbow, who is comfortably positioned and—get this—knitting already! She is not so appeased with your apology.

That's why I love it when my bag won't fit. This is the bag that I carried across concourse A, through concourses B, C, D, E and whoops, back to C, the bag I almost never got zipped back up with everything back in it after they had to check my shampoo because I must have surely put a meth lab in that little bottle, and the bag I successfully fit in the bathroom and shut the stall door after numerous tries, and then stood there looking at the door wondering if I could possibly get in there also. While everyone else is apprehensive thinking he'll never see his bag again, I say, "Here, pick mine! Put a pink tag on it, and if I never see it again, it will be too soon."

After making it to my seat, it is here that I sometimes find out I'm sitting by the emergency exit door. They ask me if I'm aware I'm sitting here, if I'm willing to help other passengers, and if I understand what to do. I nod on the outside, and think on the inside, "You are all going to die."

All right, wheels up, so let's get to the important stuff. Bring on the refreshment cart. How is it I had nothing but a purse, and I brushed against someone from all 192 countries, and this steward can get down the aisle with a hot dog stand? Only this one just comes with snack-size (if you're a guppy) pretzel bags and soda. Even though I'm okay with flying, my stomach isn't, so I'm really eager for the soda because the carbonated stuff sometimes helps.

And sometimes it doesn't. Feeling more and more queasy last time, I checked numerous times to make sure I had the necessary complementary bag in the pouch in front of me. It wasn't there. Oh, it wasn't there. Three questions came quickly to mind: (1) Why me? (2) Uh-oh, what happened in this seat on the last flight? and (3) I'm paying how much to go through this? At this point, I began praying not only for myself, but for the guy next to me.

And then a thought occurred to me that hadn't before. Why does that row across from me have only one seat, and this one has two? Doesn't that defy every law of physics that I was supposed to learn in twelfth grade? Are we flying lopsided? Did they think this through?

When I get to the ground, I realize surely my prayers have been answered. I just arrived safely on a plane that had basic design flaws, a dead battery, and a pilot that couldn't get down the down escalator without mechanical problems. It's true that the age of miracles is over, but I can't help but think I just got a near-lethal injection of providence.

6

IF MAMA AIN'T HAPPY,
Stick Her on That JOY Bus!

Stubbornness or Submission

Maybe you gave birth to one. If you didn't, sing the "Hallelujah Chorus" one time more than the rest of us. James Dobson called her "the strong-willed child" in his book by that title in 1978. The truth is, all of us are born with a strong will. We all came out screaming, "I want it now." But there is a creature that carries it further than the rest of us. Some metals bend under pressure. With some it takes heat, and some have to be chiseled slowly with the toughest of tools. Some are just unmalleable.

Meet Mattianne. She was born with beautiful eyes, bushy black hair, and more kickback than a 12-gauge shotgun. Early on, she was maternal in nature, caring for her dolls and fluffy bears, gently rocking her younger siblings, and as the years passed by, dozens of little ones she hardly knew would reach for her, talk to her in gibberish, and sleep on her shoulder. How could a Mary Poppins in capri pants and a ponytail have had such a fiercely independent start? She gave renewed energy to the song "Iowa Stubborn," and she was in Alabama. Friends would encourage me by saying that this strong will would eventually morph into leadership when channeled in the right direction. It might have been true, but I was weary of hearing it. In fact, I was just weary, period.

Don't get me wrong; I cherished the preschool years. As with her siblings, I valued the time. I mentally recorded the laughter, the sweaty kisses, and flowery weeds picked with care. She was good. She was really good. But there is a poem by Henry Wadsworth Longfellow that says:

> There was a little girl,
> Who had a little curl,
> Right in the middle of her forehead.
> When she was good,
> She was very good indeed,
> But when she was bad she was horrid.

I didn't need CliffsNotes to get me through that piece of literature. I had a live demonstration. I, like every other mother, had all the answers to parenting until I became one. And while I did, and still do, believe in strict discipline, I found that all the tried-and-true methods were now more trying than true. We talked, we spanked, we talked some more, we inflicted consequences, but she still wasn't signing the treaty. The more delicately the plans were detailed for the day or the more onlookers we had, the grander the stand-off.

I wasn't giving in. That would be detrimental to her future. She wasn't giving in. That would be a betrayal of her core self. And so I remember on more than one occasion, while the rest of the family enjoyed—*enjoyed* is probably a strong word as I could only imagine my husband trying to juggle the other three at a dinner table with liquids and dress clothes—a meal in a restaurant, Mattianne and I sat in a hot minivan because she would not meet the terms of a truce. The same thing happened with extended family game night. I never got to lay down the first Scrabble tile. I had to deal with the stubborn child.

I can't even remember what the infraction was on any of these occasions. But this I know: The stubbornness was all that lay in the way of the joy. It usually is.

Notice that the one who was determined to plow her own way was now enclosed in a small space, and separated from those enjoying the day. Stubbornness does that. It truly imprisons us.

The Whisper of Submission

On the other hand, we think that our freedom is being challenged through the call to submission. Why would we want to submit our will to someone else's? We'd rather be free to forge our own trails. Somehow those trails lead to dead ends. When the world revolves around us, it's a very small world closing in on us. But when we reverse roles, and put others' wants and needs up front, we experience the freedom to explore the wide-open joy God has in store for us. There is no ceiling or wall to joy when it comes from considering others.

But submission is the word that we're almost afraid to say out loud. Why? Because it's counter to culture. It really has more to do with our mindset than our actions. And it is certainly not the mindset of the world. Read Romans 8:5–7 with me:

> For those who live according to the flesh set their minds on the things of the flesh, but those who live according to the Spirit set their minds on the things of the Spirit. For to set the mind on the flesh is death, but to set the mind on the Spirit is life and peace. For the mind that is set on the flesh is hostile to God, for it does not submit to God's law; indeed, it cannot.

There are two ways of living here based on two ways of thinking: two mindsets. One of those is set on its own ways. Sounds like stubbornness. The other is set on the things of the Spirit. We get a list of some of those "things" in Galatians 5:22–23: "Love, joy, peace, patience, kindness, goodness, faithfulness, gentleness, self-control."

The Link with Christianity

We start with two mindsets which lead to two results. One is death, and one is life and peace. Isn't it interesting that by yielding our will, patiently persevering through gentleness and holding ourselves back in self-control, we get what every person wants deep down: life and peace?

With two mindsets and two results, there emerge two attitudes: "For the mind that is set on the flesh is hostile to God, for it does not submit to God's law; indeed, it cannot." There's your stand-off. There's the stubborn mule.

Cannot is a strong word, huh? It is because it's chained to a strong will. We pretend that submission is not a big deal but maybe just a little footnote, when in reality it is linked so solidly with Christianity that you cannot have one without the other. Cannot.

Submission to our elders, submission to our government, submission to our husbands, and submission to one another (individuals) becomes less of a debate when we first completely resign the mindset on the flesh, our own desires, break down the wall of hostility to God, and experience life and peace.

Beyond Equality: The Feminist Movement

The feminist movement is one that has robbed us of that joy. I love feminism, in that I love God's elevation of the woman and her soul. I happen to be a female, and I wouldn't have it any other way. Women are to be respected, valued, and esteemed.

But the feminist movement has gone beyond equality—of course we are equal!—and exalts only the female as the strong, the powerful, and the proud. At its core, it casts off submission of any kind, except to its own notions, but specifically it disdains men in any kind of respectable light. It mocks God's design from the beginning, that these two, male and female, *complete* one another; not *compete with* one another.

The movement has been vocal through decades if not a century, and we have heard it so much that it has permeated our thinking, maybe even our mindset. Within the church, we have second-guessed New Testament instruction and have muddied the waters to the point that when we hear the word submission, we cringe.

But remember, while there is more than one time when the Spirit directs New Testament writers to address a wife's submission to her husband, that is not the whole of submission. Not by far. Submission is our very mindset. It includes the gamut of our lives. Like what?

Submission to Scripture

Enthusiasm about spiritual matters is great but not enough. In Romans 10, Paul says that he can attest to Israel's zeal, but it's not based on knowledge (v. 2). He then describes that since these people didn't know about God's righteousness, they set about to establish their own. Sound familiar?

People are full of ideas about how to glorify God in worship, communicate acceptance of all behaviors, and marry Christianity to all forms of religion. The problem is, as the text in Romans points out, those are our own ideas, and not God's. "For, being ignorant of the righteousness of God, and seeking to establish their own, they did not submit to God's righteousness" (Rom. 10:3).

This lack of submission resulted from a lack of knowledge. People are doing seemingly innocent, yet wrong things because they fail in reading scripture, our source of knowledge about God's righteousness. We're making it up as we go along. It seems good to us, so why not? Isn't that the same reasoning of the strong-willed toddler? I want to do it, so why not?

> *For, being ignorant of the righteousness of God, and seeking to establish their own, they did not submit to God's righteousness (Rom. 10:3).*

Submission to Government

The Christian life is an overcoming one. We overcome temptations. We overcome our past. And in the last verse of Romans 12, we overcome evil with good (v. 21). Without the chapter division, the very next sentence says, "Let every person be subject to the governing authorities" (Rom. 13:1).

Right before Romans 12:21, we have instruction to help our enemies out with every physical need. Right after Romans 12:21, we have instruction to submit to our government. In both activities, a cooperative spirit just has to be conspicuous to those outside of Christ. They have to notice that kind of behavior because it is in stark contrast to the rest of the world. It is an overcoming spirit.

I sometimes hear people say that they would respect the government if it would only be respectable. Don't forget the government Paul lived under when the Holy Spirit inspired this directive. The emperor at the time is described by History.com in the following manner:

> Perhaps the most infamous of Rome's emperors, Nero Claudius Caesar (AD 37–68) ruled Rome from AD 54 until his death by suicide fourteen years later. He is best known for his debaucheries, political murders, persecution of Christians and a passion for music that led to the probably apocryphal rumor that Nero "fiddled" while Rome burned during the great fire of AD 64."

It seems that under such an evil reign, Paul's every "blog and podcast" would have been a political rant for a return to decency. I'm sure he prayed for it, but while he did, he knew what Jesus told us, twice, in the same verse, "My kingdom is not of this world" (John 18:36). We should be dismayed at evil, but back to Romans 13, verse 1 is not just an offhand remark. Paul spends a hefty seven verses here explaining that God is for government, that it was his idea, and get this: "Whoever resists the authorities resists what God has appointed" (v. 2). It's true with every kind of submission. Submission to people is an extension of submission to God. So the conclusion drawn in Romans 13 is that we should be in subjection for two basic reasons: (1) If we don't, we're going to have to fear the wrath of God, and (2) If we don't, we're going to have to live with a guilty conscience (v. 5).

In fact, 1 Peter 2:17 places "honor the emperor" immediately after "fear God." And 1 Timothy 2 allows us to see just how we are to do it. It's a prayer issue, but Paul doesn't just leave us with the broad suggestion of prayer. He gets pretty specific.

Are our leaders antagonistic toward righteousness? Beg (supplicate)! Are times critical for them, and for us? Pray! Are their decisions paramount in influence for our generation and those to come? Make intercession!

What? How can I intercede? How can I intervene? Christ is the mediator between God and man. This very text says so in verse 5, and yet in verse 1, it requires that four kinds of communication from man to God be made, and one of them is intercession! There is a sense in which we make intercession by coming to God on behalf of others. We cannot change things, but prayer to and through the one who does change things accomplishes much.

> *Therefore, confess your sins to one another and pray for one another, that you may be healed. The prayer of a righteous person has great power as it is working (James 5:16).*

And then there is that last form of prayer mentioned in 1 Timothy 2:1: thanksgiving. How long has it been since you thanked God for a government leader, especially one like Nero? And yet the very next phrase, after these four types of prayer are mentioned, is that they are "for all men, kings and *all* who are in high positions."

We tend to want to be thankful for, and submissive to, the good-guy brand of president, senator, mayor, and down the line. But "all" is an entirely thorough word. Don't miss the result though, "that we may live a peaceful and quiet life." I grew up hearing, "I can't win for losing," but I'm coming to realize that with the submission kind of losing, I win by losing every time.

There is one exception to our submission to the government. There is an exception to our submission to anyone. And that's stated best by Peter and the apostles when they said,

> *We must obey God rather than men (Acts 5:29).*

Even so, they chose rejoicing over revolution when they were beaten and released (Acts 5:40–42).

Submission in the Church

When our children were very young, we selected a group of short verses to put to memory, ones we thought they could master before they could read. One of these was 1 Timothy 2:11, nine words in the NKJV. They got eight of them right, but it didn't quite carry the meaning of the original text when my daughter announced loudly, "Let the woman learn in silence with all seduction," but it may have rung truer in the actual assembly once or twice when I couldn't tell if a sister was wearing a long shirt or a short dress, but either way, someone forgot her pants.

Actually, though my daughter didn't understand it at the time, that thought of seduction is pulled into the text, but it's the lack thereof. Titus 2 and 1 Timothy 2 give us a vivid picture of who we are to be as God's women: the loveliness and modesty of our dress; the quiet, learning spirit; and the magnanimous responsibility of shaping little fireballs into godly men and women.

Someone forgot her pants.

Don't miss it. Among the things we can compare it to would be a conversation like this:

"Do you drive race cars?"

"No, I build them."

God didn't give us as women the role of being preachers and elders, but he entrusted us with the confidence to build them.

In another chapter of this book, I talk about not throwing away your confidence (Heb. 10:35). While not the primary application there, I think it makes an excellent one here. Why would we throw away such a beautiful confidence that God bestows on us because we refuse to submit?

Submission to Elders

And why not? Now that we have studied thus far that at the very core of Christianity lies the complete mindset of submission, why would we stumble over submission within Christ's own body, the church (Col. 1:18)? It seems there couldn't be a wider miss of the mark than to miss submission when it pertains to yielding to those overseeing the very body we are part of. While this can be dangerous in man-made religions where the power-hungry can enjoy control over the vulnerable, God thoroughly laid out guidelines in 1 Timothy 3 and Titus 1 for the careful selection of those who would lovingly shepherd his flock.

"I'd hate to teach that kid."

I don't know about you, but I need help walking the straight and narrow some days. Most. Okay, all! So many things to trip up on seem to fall in my path, so many snares, and so many distractions to lure me away. Wouldn't it be nice if I could just have another person, a team of people really, to watch out for me? Good news! Hebrews 13:17 tells us that these elders, these leaders, watch for our souls. In turn, I can make their job joyful or painful.

As an analogy, my mother was a teacher to the core. She watched over children's minds and their future. She loved it, coming home telling stories of the light-bulb moments, the wins and the do-overs, and the hilarious moments in between. She taught with joy. But I remember once, sitting in the car outside of the grocery store, waiting for Daddy to return with a gallon of milk and a pack of toilet paper, we watched a little boy, about ten, hair matted and sporting a skull-and-crossbones shirt, coming down the sidewalk. He turned around and wagged his head at his mother. We couldn't hear what he said, but you could tell it was next to the word *smart aleck* in the dictionary. He then strutted about three feet in front of her, pretty sure that he owned not only the Dr Pepper in his hand, but the world that went with it. And my mother said something I'd never heard her say before: "I'd hate to teach that kid."

What brought about this sudden reversal in a woman who lived to instill knowledge and values in children's minds? The obvious attitude of the boy we were viewing through the windshield. He would not have been submissive, and therefore, her job would have been a trial, and most likely a failure. Where teaching was usually a joy, in this case it would have been trying, burdensome, tiring. Take a second look at this passage:

> *Obey your leaders and submit to them,*
> *for they are keeping watch over your souls,*
> *as those who will have to give an account.*
> *Let them do this with joy and not with groaning,*
> *for that would be of no advantage to you*
> *(Heb. 13:17).*

Some Christians glory in trying to have the upper hand, the advantage, in dealing with church elders. Ultimatums are sometimes given about where we'll go to church from now on or how much we'll give. Make no mistake—a pretty word for sin here—there is no advantage in having the advantage. The New King James Version says plainly, "that would be unprofitable for you."

Submission to Your Husband

There are a number of New Testament passages that spell out submission to our husbands (1 Pet. 3:1; 1 Cor. 11:3; Col. 3:18), but my favorite is Ephesians 5. While for hundreds of years, women have asked why, I think these verses give a solid "because." Here it is:

> *Wives, submit to your own husbands, as to the Lord. For the husband is the head of the wife even as Christ is the head of the church, his body, and is himself its Savior. Now as the church submits to Christ, so also wives should submit in everything to their husbands* (Eph. 5:22–24).

This is a trust test. First of all, it requires that we trust God, no matter how much our spirit within us wants to kick, no matter if it makes perfect sense to us or not. It is God's command, and as with so many of the Old Testament commands that he finished with "I am the Lord," we follow this command in the New Testament just because he still is the Lord.

Second, it requires fully entrusting our family lives to our husbands within God's will. This is paramount. Our men want to be trusted. They have an inbuilt desire to be respected which makes them good leaders if we don't throw those ideals of trust and respect to the side. That's why God is so serious about this. It's really for our good, and not our detriment. Notice, he even says to submit to our own husbands, as to the Lord. That's not a little amount. That's not just a hefty amount. That's an all-or-nothing amount!

Husbands: Die for Your Wives

Thank God it's not a one-way street. God looks at us, as his daughters, in this scenario and basically says, "You! You submit to him." And then he turns to his sons, and says, "You! You die for her!" Look at the counterpart scripture to the men: "Husbands, love your wives, as Christ loved the church and gave himself up for her" (Eph. 5:25).

The Lie

No one's a doormat. No one's self-esteem is at risk. Everyone is valued here in the perfect plan as only God could plan it.

But still, marriage is one of Satan's favorite targets because if he can destroy it, there will be innocent and helpless victims, and he rejoices in a bleak future for them. So because he never veers far from his target, he uses his same old strategy since Genesis 3—the lie. Saying the direct opposite of what God has made clear, and making it somehow sound true.

Submission to husbands just is not a big deal. That's the lie, even though the passage we just looked at says we should submit "as to the Lord." We laugh at that, and when possible, ignore it. Satan puts a "not" right before the word *submit* in Ephesians 5:24 just as certainly as he put it before *surely die* in Genesis 3:4.

Who's the Boss?

The married Christian woman, more often than should be the case, believes she can be pleasing to God and an upstanding citizen of heaven (Phil. 3:20) through a number of accolades from organizing a medical missions campaign to writing and coordinating ten years worth of curriculum, but all the while returning home where she's always the boss and rarely yields. Is it the case that, even in the midst of good works, we play out our days and nights just like the world tells us to?

We've got to trust God's protocol.

I'm glad to be on the exit side of a TV era where every man on any sitcom or toothpaste commercial was the dumbest and laziest creature alive, and the women had to take up all the slack. Thankfully, the responsible husbands and dads are back in vogue. TV now shows them engaged with their young children, and there's something precious about that which I believe God smiles on. But notice, the roles are reversed as the dad drives the vacuum cleaner while waiting for the mom to show up in time for the dinner they've cooked, or they wave as she rushes out the door.

I heard a radio call-in show where the host was advising the female caller to allow her husband to have a few responsibilities—give him some things he can handle.

My husband can handle, with God's help and grace, what God entrusts him with, and that's the care and leadership of this home. I'm not in the position to grant him a few chores, but to rely on him to take the stern, knowing he would die before allowing those souls in his home to shipwreck.

Redesign Is Blasphemy

We have, as a society and maybe as a church, adopted a "whatever" attitude about the home. "Whatever" attitudes always lack direction, and trips without direction rarely land in safe or happy destinations. God does want us to be happy, but we've got to trust his protocol.

It's interesting that Titus 2:4–5 tells us that if the older women teach the younger women how to work at home and to love their husbands, then the word of God will not be reviled (ESV) or blasphemed (NKJV and others). What's the converse of that truth? It just follows that if we redesign the home and teach our younger generation that it really doesn't matter, the result *is* blasphemy.

If submission seems a trivial thing, what about blasphemy? Where does that rank? The two are interrelated in significance.

Submission to One Another

When my sister was in the first grade, her teacher tried to tell her she was writing her letters wrong. She gently held Sami's hand around the pencil, and said, "If you point your pencil in this direction, and draw a line here, you can make a capital E like you're supposed to." Sami looked at the teacher's letter, pondered it for a moment and said, "Well, you can make yours like that. I'm going to make mine this way."

We all want to do it our way, but the bottom line is, we're a lot happier if we submit to one another. It's just the heart of who we are as disciples. Remember that "mountainside" chapter of this book? We're just happy when we're meek. In 1 Peter 5, the author talks a little about submission specifics, but then gives this broad command:

> *Clothe yourselves, all of you, with humility toward one another, for "God opposes the proud but gives grace to the humble." Humble yourselves, therefore, under the mighty hand of God so that at the proper time he may exalt you*
> *(1 Pet. 5:5–6).*

Do you know what brings up the rear of this verse? It's an all-time favorite. It probably comes to your mind every single day; I know it does mine. Verse 7 says, "Casting all your anxieties on him, because he cares for you." God will stick to his end of the deal; will we stick to ours? Are we willing to submit to one another as we rely on God to fully shoulder all of our anxieties? It looks like, with the side-by-side nature of the passage, these two go hand in hand. If we trust him with our problems, we're going to have to trust his instruction for us to give up that strong will and submit to others.

We're going to have to quit trying to outdo each other, and well, outdo each other. "Love one another with brotherly affection. Outdo one another in showing honor" (Rom. 12:10). It's the only time the word *outdo* is used in the Bible, at least in this translation, and it's used in the context of submission.

Submit. It's that bottom oval button at the end of every curbside order, every online purchase, and every complicated registration form. It sounds simple, but it almost never goes through on the first try. We try again. We see problems, red type that tells us we did something wrong. Pay close attention to the red type. Jesus' own words have become synonymous with the red type in the Bibles we hold. They'll tell us not only what we're doing wrong but how to make it right. Since all submission falls under our willingness to first submit to God, the submit button does not, cannot work if we ignore the red type, or any type, really, since all scripture is God-inspired (2 Tim. 3:16).

Perfect Submission

For all the frustration that a non-working submit button brings, there is such a sigh of relief when we finally see the screen come up that says "successfully submitted." There is always a sigh of relief with godly submission. It's a much happier route than the kicking and screaming one.

For that very reason, one of my favorite hymns is an ancient one we call "Blessed Assurance." There is nothing that surpasses the assurance of knowing we are in Christ, sins forgiven, heavenward bound. But there is a particular specific thought within this hymn that ties together everything I've been trying to communicate in this chapter. To think, I could have done it in fourteen words:

> Perfect submission, all is at rest,
> I, in my Savior, am happy and blest.

Submission. Rest. Happiness. We probably just thought it was a gimmick in the seventies when every church had a bus, and every bus had the letters JOY on the side of it. Maybe the letters should have read CSW since most of the joy we got was from C for candy, S for hitting speed bumps, and W for those windows that latched and unlatched as we prepared for the "World Window Sliding Up and Down" quarterfinals. But we knew what the JOY acronym was about: *Jesus first. Others second. Yourself last.* Joy was easier to spell than submission, but that's what it was all about. That joy that comes from putting others ahead of yourself.

So if Mama ain't happy, stick her on that JOY bus!

Outdo one another in showing honor
(Rom. 12:10).

 # If You're Happy, You Will Know It

1. Do you have a strong-willed child? If you are a mother navigating the early childhood years, this week ask a woman you trust, who has raised her children, what thing was the most valuable in bringing a child's will under subjection. If you have already raised a strong-willed child, befriend, through a special act this week, and hopefully weeks to come, a young mother who's going through that trying process.

2. Considering that in God's ideal plan, the wife submits, as to the Lord, and the husband loves, to the point of dying for her, who is expected to give up more? There may not be a right or wrong answer here, but it's a compelling thought question.

3. Read Titus 2:5 in a number of translations. There are about five ideas there that must be taught, or else God's word will be dishonored or blasphemed. From that list, which of these do you think is the most ignored?

4. Have a notepad or a texting app open as you have a few opportunities to watch TV this week. Make a note when you see a man weakly cowering to his wife, whether on a comical commercial or an episode of a series. What's your tally?

5. If you're a married woman, make a special effort to respect your husband this week. Every day choose something that he does right, even a small thing, even if you have to think awhile to come up with it, and tell him you respect him for it.

6. Consider the placement of 1 Peter 5:7 right after the two preceding verses. Is there something in submission and humility that might trigger the anxiety in verse 7? Is there some power struggle that is hard to let go of, and the thought of doing so is stirring anxiety? Considering the promise in verse 7, write what you fear most. Copy verse 7 right after what you wrote, and then go back and cross out what was written before the verse was written. God can handle it for you.

Happy Trails

And speaking of restaurants . . .

I wish I didn't have to go to court all the time. Food court, that is. We all thought it was a great idea in the eighties. It mooted all the commercials where the family sits in the car and tries to pick a restaurant. It ruined all the preachers' and motivational speakers' number one illustration about how to come to an agreement as a family.

And we thought it was cheap. That was the main thing. Everyone could get what they wanted, and four dollars here and five-fifty there sounded a whole lot better than thirty-nine. Not to mention we could save time by everyone ordering at once.

But the choosing part became more grueling than ever. Now, instead of sitting in a car in front of the dry cleaners because your husband has pulled over and said, "I am not driving one more centimeter until someone in this vehicle decides," we can actually hold the argument in the most public place in town. At this point, people actually try to step in and help the family decide. "Free Sample?" they call. Syrup-y meat pieces shaped incredibly like Paraguay dangle from toothpicks. We take them because they're free and keep moving while the band plays, "White rice and a side for three-ninety-nine."

Then at the end of the circuit, I say "You know what? I've eaten all this Paraguay-shaped chicken. I'm not really hungry anymore. I think I'm good." This is precisely why I'm not a vegetarian.

But no one else seems to feel this way—full. So we have one that wants pizza, one that wants a steak sandwich, one that wants chili-cheese chips, one for Paraguay pieces, and one that says, "Can I just get an egg roll here and cheese fries way over there and macaroni two blocks down?" This is when we realize, between the six of us, we have one debit card and sixty-two cents. So we begin an ordering marathon. "Take the debit card to the sub place; bring me the receipt. Then Abram can go to the pizza line, which currently wraps around the equator twice, and then the rest of us can order next January. Doesn't anybody want regular American chicken nuggets? Anyone? Anyone?"

I ask in pleading tones because we know now the established fact that the drinks at the American chicken nugget place are a full thirty cents lower than anywhere else in this phenomenally expensive mall food market. But no one goes for this, so we will now send the debit card to the ninth line to get the drinks.

Wasn't Watergate faster than this? Did the Thirty Years War even take this long?

Watch out for the clean-up crew! They're serious, circulating through the tables in matching shirts with dustpans, and trying to catch you off guard. One trip to the bathroom, one sprint to the napkin dispenser, one turn to see if the equator has shortened, and it's gone. They can wipe out six drinks and all of Paraguay in the blink of an eye. And you yell, "Don't! That drink is two dollars and sixteen cents!" And they smile and say, "Limpie las tablas" which must be translated, "Ha ha, you save time and money at the Cracker Barrel."

But there is one more ludicrous touch to this entire scenario that I would like to address. There, in the middle of this overpriced chaos, there is a seemingly serene attraction. Someone has moved a carousel inside . . . in here . . . in the mall. I must admit it's inviting, with it's white lights and ornate nineteenth-century horses. I also must admit it's three dollars a kid. The sign says it doesn't take debit cards, so I count the sixty-two cents again.

I know, I know, there's that nearby anytime machine that gives you cash for a small transaction fee. Small is a relative word that can sometimes mean big, such as "I have a small swimming pool" or "We are at war with a small country" or "I am having a small bankruptcy problem."

"A horse, a horse . . . My kingdom for a horse." Or at least my would-be new couch pillows. I wave sixty-four times at the four of them, which of course, works up an appetite.

Anybody sell dessert for sixty-two cents?

7

IF MAMA AIN'T HAPPY,
Give Her Another Measuring Stick

Self-Righteous or Reliant

There would only be three finalists. The little boys, all age eight, sat biting their nails and swinging legs that would not quite reach from the chairs to the floor. They had all done their best, and now there was no more to do but wait . . . and wait . . . and wait . . . for the dreaded announcement. They had each sung a song before a panel of judges, and each couldn't help but, in his heart, compare himself to the others. Each was convinced he was hands down the best; it's a very narcissistic age. But only three could be finalists, and only those three would get to stay and sing again for the next tier of competition.

It was the first rodeo for most of them, and while they seemed to understand the rules, it turned out that Junior, the little boy we were there to cheer on and/or console, wasn't too clear on what was going on. The announcement was made, his name wasn't in it, and our stomachs took a dive while our faces tried to make congratulatory expressions for the others. But Junior wasn't even a little disappointed. He stood up and strutted toward us. "I did *real* good," he crowed. "They made three of the boys stay and do theirs again. But not me, I got it right the first time!"

Some days are like that. Sometimes we compare ourselves to others, and perceiving that they've done worse than we have, we're happy. That's the wrong kind of happy, people! It's called self-righteousness, and God might let it slide when you're eight, but by the time we're upwards of remembering the first *American Idol* season, we ought to do better.

Take the Whole "Self" Out

Righteousness is good. I mean, very good. It sits on the opposite side of the equal sign with good. Righteousness exalts a nation (Prov. 14:34), it forges the paths God leads us in (Ps. 23:3), and it's the first thing we seek every day before coffee (Matt. 6:33). But stick that word *self* in front of it, and everything changes. It's like putting *raw* in front of shrimp, *boiled* in front of peanuts, and *white* in front of chocolate. We've moved from excellence to despair in one syllable.

If you're easing into the territory of self-righteousness, despair! There's nothing good there. Raise your hand if you're self-righteous. Anyone? I doubt it. The very fact that you're on page _____ of a study of Bible topics indicates you're interested in righteousness, and not the "self" kind. But even among the most studious and hard-working of Christians, we need to be on guard against this beast. I say that because I believe if it happened to close followers like Peter, it can happen to any of us. Look at Matthew 26:33: Peter answered Jesus, "Though they all fall away because of you, I will never fall away." Two things trouble me in his statement. The first is that he starts out focusing on the wrong that other people are doing in comparison to his own plans. The second is his use of the word *never*.

Measuring Wrong

Self-righteousness always uses the wrong measuring stick. Measuring wrong produces disastrous results. Once my mother, trying to parallel park on the downtown streets of Birmingham, asked for help from the only person available, a four-year-old. She asked my sister Sami, "How much room do I have back there before I hit the other car?" Sami raised her eyes barely over the back dash, and said, "You have . . . three . . . ketchup bottles." We can get in a lot of trouble measuring like that. Sami was excused; she hadn't even started kindergarten. She could hardly count to twelve, much less know that's how many inches were in a foot—something she only knew about when it came to kicking me.

I once had an antique cookbook typed up before there was a fraction key on the keyboard—typewriter, really. And so where it meant ¾ of a cup of flour, I thought it said 3–4 cups, so I put 3½ cups for safe measure (but terrible cookies). There's no such thing as safe measure when it's wrong measure.

You can't measure distances with ketchup bottles, and you can't measure God's acceptance of your life with the "Well, it's better than hers" stick.

It's what Peter did. After looking at everyone else and deciding they would all probably do the wrong thing, he then boasted that he never would. He was oozing self-righteousness from every pore, and that's when it all began to fall apart for him. When this happens, we've just bet the whole bank on someone we know is prone to failure, and fear takes over as it did for Peter. He had plenty to fear when he watched his Lord and friend as he was arrested and led away for a cruel beating. Now, he stood right next to those accusing him of being Jesus' friend. He was fearful.

Self-Exam

Self-righteous moments look like pride on the outside but stink with fear on the inside. They don't make for happy memories.

On the other hand, full reliance on God stacks days into happy calendars. Knowing, believing, and admitting our worthlessness, helplessness, and condemnation if not for his grace, we just keep on walking in the light, and with every stumble we're a little more grateful for that light, that grace, and that guiding outreached hand. We have no claim to providing a bit of the light, but we sure are grateful to be walking in it.

If Mama ain't happy, which kind of righteousness is she hanging on to? If someone like Peter could dabble in self-righteousness until he denied the Lord, we need a constant self-examination to make sure we never venture into that camp (or campfire).

> *He saved us, not because of works done by us in righteousness, but according to his own mercy (Titus 3:5).*

Exam Section 1. Humanities: Is There an Obsession with the Wrong in Other People?

In Luke 18:9–14, Jesus addresses our topic. It begins, "He also told this parable to some who trusted in themselves that they were righteous, and treated others with contempt" (v. 9). There's a summation of the problem we have in the church a couple of thousand years later. Trust and treat, and it's not a parking lot candy raid in October. That's a different problem.

This one has to do with trusting ourselves. *Trust* is a strong word, and Peter had plenty of it. "I'll never . . . " It's the wrong way to start a sentence. God will never let us down when we trust in him, but people are prone to let us down, especially the one in the mirror.

Treat is the other pivotal word. It's a sad condition to have contempt for a person made in the image of God, but it's even worse to act on that contempt and treat people as if they are substandard.

Paul, in the second letter to the Corinthians, basically says, "You just don't get it." Literally, he says, "They are without understanding" (10:12). Who is? When? "Everyone is when they measure themselves by one another and compare themselves with one another." There's that broken measuring stick again.

Exam Section 2. Spelling: Can We Get Past "I"?

Let's explore further.

> Two men went up into the temple to pray, one a Pharisee and the other a tax collector. The Pharisee, standing by himself, prayed thus: "God, I thank you that I am not like other men, extortioners, unjust, adulterers, or even like this tax collector. I fast twice a week; I give tithes of all that I get" (Luke 18:11–12).

Four times, he used the "I" word. We call that "full of himself." When you're full of yourself, you're at maximum capacity. God won't fit. In fact, in the New King James Version, verse 11 reads, "The Pharisee stood and prayed thus with himself," rather than, "standing by himself, prayed." His prayer was just a big selfie. He was so far into self that he was having a conversation with his favorite person. Either translation isn't a great reflection on his prayer life—one indicates his prayer wasn't Godward, and the other indicates he was too good to pray with the rest of us.

Imagine! Some nerve! I'm glad I would never be like that Pharisee—Wait! Did I just . . . ? See what I mean? It's easier for good people to fall into self-righteousness than we might realize. All we have to do is start comparing ourselves to other people, and suddenly we're walking around with a one-by-four piece of lumber sticking out of our pupil (Matt. 7:3–5).

God, I thank you that I am not like other men (Luke 18:11).

Exam Section 3. Word Limit: Knowing When to Quit

I read a Facebook post some time back, and it said something like, "Today, at the grocery store, I was so proud when my daughter quickly grabbed the door, and held it open for an elderly man who was moving a little slowly."

It was a sweet post. It should have ended there. But instead, it went on to say, "I've noticed that a lot of young people do not take the time to open doors for older people."

Uh-oh, this crossed the line into comparing ourselves with other people instead of being amazed at God's goodness. When our children shine the brightest, it's still far more about what God has done than anything we have done. And so, of course, next, it began to fall apart.

The next sentence read, "This is because we have been careful to teach our children to have respect and do kind deeds."

Upon reading that, I immediately thought, "I thank thee that I am not like other men." I can't help it; my mind thinks in the King James Version. The more we rattle on about what other people don't do, and what we do, the more we ease from righteousness into self-righteousness. Let's quit with, I saw someone do a good thing; isn't God good?

Exam Section 4. Retaining: Do We Remember Where We Came From?

In case we get lifted up with pride, let us never forget the slop our pigpen lives were in before coming to Christ. It doesn't mean we revisit the past; it means we are so thankful we don't have to.

> But the tax collector, standing far off, would not even lift up his eyes to heaven, but beat his breast, saying, "God, be merciful to me, a sinner!" I tell you, this man went down to his house justified, rather than the other. For everyone who exalts himself will be humbled, but the one who humbles himself will be exalted (Luke 18:13–14).

I guess one could argue that it's not too happy to be looking at the ground, beating your breast and announcing your failures. But it's pretty happy to go to your house justified because you serve a great, merciful God. A reflection on what God has done for me, a miserable sinner (1 Tim. 1:15 KJV), takes me all the way to the house with renewed celebration over God's unfathomable, rich grace.

Exam Section 5. Mythology: We Somehow Did This Ourselves.

We remember a story in Numbers 20 when Moses struck the rock after he had been told to speak to it. Disobedience was the issue we usually recall, but it wasn't the only issue. If Peter's not an alarming example of the caliber of person who can fall into self-righteousness, how about someone with the meekness of Moses? But he had set this meekness aside in the rock-striking episode. Look at verse 10: "Then Moses and Aaron gathered the assembly together before the rock, and he said to them, 'Hear now, you rebels: shall we bring water for you out of this rock?'"

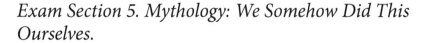

Disobedience was the issue.

First, he made it clear that he was looking at the problems within the other guys. It was justified to the degree that the Israelites' ungrateful attitudes were repulsive, but his focus on their wrong fed, in this case, an overestimation of self instead of Moses' usual interceding spirit (Exod. 32:32). He then had the gall to say, "Shall we bring water for you out of this rock?" Be clear; Moses and Aaron had never brought water out of a rock. Only God can do that.

Be clear; we can never cause water to place a soul inside the Rock washing away all sin. Only God can do that. So why would we ever gloat over any of our own righteousness, since someone else has paid the price? Only God can do that.

The Unity Ruler

Which brings us to the right measuring stick. We have to examine ourselves. We have to evaluate our soul's condition, but if we don't use the comparison stick, which one do we use? The unity one. We help each other to grow up into one beautiful ideal. In Ephesians 4, Paul explains that Christ's plan was for us to work together, with many different talents and roles, but with one goal.

> *Until we all attain to the unity of the faith*
> *and of the knowledge of the Son of God,*
> *to mature manhood, to the measure of the*
> *stature of the fullness of Christ*
> *(Eph. 4:13).*

When I stand on my best ballerina tiptoes, I cannot get there. But when I begin to work together with my sisters, to lift others up on my shoulders, and they brace me from falling back down, together we believe and we know ("the faith and of the knowledge") that the Son of God is growing us into who he wants us to be—"the measure of the stature of the fullness of Christ."

His lips quivered as his voice broke.

What more can I say? How can we conclude this chapter? Nothing does justice to the righteousness of God, and there are no words for my worthlessness without him. So I'll just tell you what happened last night.

Last night marked the first time that the saints at my home congregation, Mastin Lake, could meet together again, as the stay-at-home orders during the coronavirus threat were finally lifted. It had been eight weeks, we wore masks that couldn't conceal big smiles, we sat six feet apart when our hearts weren't six inches apart, and we spent the whole time, the whole hour, in prayer.

As one of the men approached the podium, he was a spiritual giant to me—you know, like one of those who "seemed to be pillars" in the church in Galatians 2:9. As he began to speak before the prayer, to elaborate on some of the situations he had on his list, he got about three words out before beginning to tremble. He got a couple more out and his lips quivered as his voice broke. And then he explained, "I'm coming to God in prayer, leading your thoughts toward God, and my heart is not perfect."

It's true. It's true for each of us. He continued to approach God in prayer, all of us with him in that, and he laid the requests out before God, with sobs and often a gap, while he mustered strength for the next supplication. And as he ended the prayer and walked back to his pew wiping his eyes, I could not help but feel that I had seen, if not been, that man who beat his chest crying, "God be merciful to me a sinner."

Aren't we glad for his mercy? Aren't we glad to return to our pew justified through no merit of our own? Aren't we just glad?

If Mama ain't happy, she might not know how glad she could be.

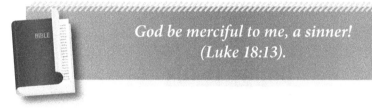

God be merciful to me, a sinner!
(Luke 18:13).

If You're Happy, You Will Know It

1. What do you think of this statement, "She can't be happy unless she can outdo someone else"? Is it possible for that to be true? In other words, can we be happy through outdoing someone else?

2. When we look at the parable of the Pharisee and the tax collector, do we see any indication of happiness in either one? Is happiness implied for either one? Is it possible that one or the other's prayer results in happiness? How do you conclude this?

3. Do you agree that both Peter and Moses had a self-righteous moment?

4. List other strong and faithful Bible characters who wandered into the territory of self-righteousness.

5. Find the passage that reveals the first time water flowed from a rock. What, if anything, is different within Moses this first time?

6. Where in scripture is Moses called meek above all other men? Why is this characteristic significant in the context of that scripture? What other times can you think of where Moses exhibited meekness?

7. Moses was taking credit (and sharing it with Aaron) for making water come from a rock. What specific instances are we guilty, by the way we phrase something without even thinking about it, of taking credit for something when it really belongs to God?

8. Find as many Bible examples as you can where tears and prayer come together.

Happy Trails

And speaking of eight-year-old finalists . . .

"Whoa!"

"This place is gigantic."

"Shh! They'll think we've never been to a convention center before."

"We haven't."

"Unless you count the Microtel."

"Exactly, but no one has to find that out if you'll all be quiet, and get that ridiculous robo-cat out of your armpit."

"Right!" My husband blurts in, "Act sophisticated! Is breakfast free?"

"Is the Easter bunny going to be able to find this place?"

It was just one of several programs throughout the brotherhood aimed at making leaders out of our little ones who flush our debit cards and leave the seat up. This worthy goal was inspired by the same guy who tried to construct a replica of the Eiffel Tower from mayonnaise.

But we go along with it. We are convicted deep in our hearts by the idea that our coming will eventually result in the breakdown of communism in Cuba through our future generation, and by the fact that the rooms are half price for the weekend.

If you don't participate in a program of this type, let me urge you to, because there's no way you can understand the dynamics until you've been there—until you too, have traveled three hundred miles with a sculpture of Elisha stuck in your hip, only to have someone fall on it and crush it as you round the hotel portico.

No one can adequately describe the intensity or the spiritual refreshment that the weekend affords. So since "adequately" rarely modifies any of my actions, I'll proceed to describe it anyway.

Arrival:

"OK, this is pretty uneventful." My son Abram looks up from his video game in the back seat.

"Do you remember . . . " my husband starts, "the group leader saying anything about what to do if the parking lot looks like a Twister game with mini-vans?"

"The mini-vans go to the right I think. The medium vans go straight ahead. The church vans pass go (but do not collect $200) after yielding to pedestrians carrying puppet stages, and the extra-large colossal vans pray really hard."

My husband takes another look at the convention center. "Look," he says, "I'm just trying to decide whether I should park in this county or the next."

Registration Check-In:

This is always at the other end of the convention center, no matter which entrance you use. This is the first time you get officially separated from the rest of your group, which is, as you know, the theme of the entire weekend. You promise to get the registration packet and meet back at the Cascades.

"Can you tell me where my group checks in and picks up the registration packet?"

"Hey! Didn't you live in my dorm? First floor? The late-night-term-paper-fireworks incident?"

"Oh yeah, it's been forever!"

Big hug.

"Do you know where group check-in is?"

"What color are you?"

"Oh this? I'm just a little green from rounding the portico with a statue of Elisha in my hip."

"No. I mean what color is your group? How many judges do you have? Did you pre-register for debate? How many non-competitive events are represented? Did you download your certificates? Do you have anything liquid, fragile, perishable, or potentially hazardous?"

"Yellow. Nine. Yes. Seventeen. Yes. Only this robo-cat and Elisha."

"Great. Then you're set. Just walk two miles to the—"

Someone taps me on the shoulder.

"Remember the campaign to the Carolinas? The late-night-funnel-cake-correspondence course episode?"

Big hug.

"Right. Do you know where I'm going?"

"What color are you?"

About fourteen miles and 3,032 hugs later, I find the art entry station.

"Tell the judges," I say as they put entry stickers on them, "this used to be Elisha, this used to be a poster with a light house, and this is not a photograph of aliens. It used to be a forest before the early-morning-hugging-cappuccino incident four miles back."

Check-In:

Somewhere, someone had an idea of reserving an extra room, just to put the food in for their congregation . . . a "hospitality" room. The term resonated with Christian service and thoughtful provision, not to mention cheap eats, and it caught on quicker than the bus program of the seventies, and with the same amount of fervor coupled with confusion. It turns out that the minivan Twister game in the parking lot was only a teaser for the cooler traffic in the foyer. I had never before felt sympathy for an elevator.

"I think we can squeeze the Coleman tank between the blue cooler and the red double-wide if we put John and Brandon on top of the bellhop. Hey! Weren't we in chorus together? Remember the fried-salad—?"

I pushed the "door close" button and opted for three flights of stairs.

Scheduling:

"All right, I'll go hear Mattianne's speech in the Lava room. You go to Abram's debate in the Roosevelt room. I met a friend from college who agreed to go with Miriam to oral Bible reading in the Flamingo room, and I'm going to drop Enoch off for song-leading in the Oregano room, and hope there's someone there with a memory of a late-night incident somewhere who can watch him."

"That's been changed," my husband said.

"What?"

"The third-grade song leading has been moved from the Oregano Room to GC20036-B7."

"Where's that?"

"What color are you?"

Navigation:

"OK, GC20036-B7 has to be right around the corner. I've found everything else including the weapons of mass destruction no one else was able to locate. They were playing hide and seek in the ice machine—OK, here's 0036-B6, it's got to be right here. Right here where there's a lovely solid plaster mocha-colored wall."

I check the program. I check the map. I check the janitorial staff.

"Please, ma'am. Can you help me find GC20036-B7?"

"Lo siento, pero no lo se" which I think can be translated "Is that an impression of Elisha in your hip?"

Only because the world is round, I eventually find B7, which is packed way over the fire code limit, and not only are John and Brandon now on top of the bellhop, but Michael and Brother Taylor also. Due to this discomfort, an announcement is made that all the two's will now go to GC20036-B8, and all the one's will move to GC20036-B23.

After the announcement, Brother Taylor says, "Are you a two or a one?"

"Lo siento, pero no lo se."

Mealtime:

Fortunately, our particular convention is located next to a super-huge-expensive-outlet mall. The sheer terror associated with ever parking again coerces the entire group to vote unanimously in favor of walking to the mall for meals.

"Let's eat in the jungle place!" someone yells.

"I eat there every night" I protest, but no one is listening.

The minors who are not legally registered to vote win out. We wait in line for a few weeks, and finally a table is cleared.

I notice and yell, "Hey, someone's leaving!"

They give me a stare, "We were voted off the island."

The food is great and the fellowship is memorable. So is the check.

Awards:

It's better than Woodstock—really. Not that I would remember. It's noisier than Christmas at Nascar Granny's. But there are no pickled beets. There are more people than at the after-Thanksgiving sale. But there is no snatching and grabbing. There are more camera flashes than at a celebrity trial. But there are no prosecutors. Amidst all the crowd and chaos, I am immersed in an indefinable sentiment. I look to my left and see a little girl who has squirmed away her dressiness. Her sash is now loose and her hair frayed. She looks at me. "I hope I win," she says. My mind races back to the Lava room, and I see a little girl confidently delivering the speech she prepared. Then my mind goes back to our living room, and I see her stumbling through it on an early round, forgetting half the text.

"I hope I win," she crosses her fingers, and I look in her eyes.

"You already have," I say.

Big hug.

Originally printed in Christian Woman *magazine, March/April 2008. Modified 2021.*

8

IF MAMA AIN'T HAPPY,
Get Her Off That Wrecking Ball!

Tearing Down or Building Up

"What does this do?" It was a normal question at the fireworks stand. One of our college professors with a doctorate in theology also apparently had a minor in explosives. The truth is, no matter how scholarly you are, and he was, or how advanced your degrees are, and they were, it's not always easy to raise a family on a Christian college salary. So it seemed all of the academicians moonlighted somewhere for the cause of higher education. This particular one made ends meet with firecracker fuses and cherry bombs each fourth of July and first of January.

His teenage boys would run the stand, and that's who was at the counter the day the question was asked, "What does this do?"

"Well, let's see," Mike answered. He thought he'd show him the nice little chase through the gravel with an array of colors and whistling sounds. That's what he thought, but he did a bit more than that, as it made contact with a box of bottle rockets, lit one of the fuses which was in a package with several other fuses, and when those exploded, they ignited nearby fuses in every direction, which continued the chain until it was a huge show with brilliant color—a full fourth of July celebration, and it went on for a full minute or so before ending with a deafening finale and a lamentable ash pile.

I never heard how the customer who asked the question reacted. I imagine if it had been me, I would have said, "Wow! I'll take one."

Build Up or Tear Down?

It takes me back to James 3:5. "So also the tongue is a small member, yet it boasts of great things. How great a forest is set ablaze by such a small fire!" How quickly the tongue can do its damage through discouragement, criticism, and belittling.

There's about as much joy in that as in sweeping up the remains of a thousand-dollar investment.

On the other hand, there is great enjoyment received from building others up. Seeing someone grow, excel, and flourish in the kingdom, and having that feeling that God allowed you to be part of it, is a high you can't get on the street. When victory comes for one, the whole team celebrates, and sometimes, all you have to do to make the team is be the one who says, "I know you can do this. I'm praying for you." We choose to be happy when we choose to build others up rather than tear them down. The opportunity comes our way in many forms. Here are some of them.

Build Up the One Who Is Down

Job's friends are actually pictured in the manual next to the subtitle "How not to do this." Job, already suffering the loss of every son and daughter, every material possession, and now his health, has just about had more than we could think humanly possible to endure. Here come the theologians. Eliphaz, for example, in chapter 15, concludes that Job's is obviously a case of just deserts for the ungodly.

Among his brazen accusations he conjures, "The wicked man writhes in pain all his days, through all the years that are laid up for the ruthless." Paraphrased, it sounds just like, "Let me tell you why you're writhing in pain, Job. It's because you're wicked and ruthless. There, I hope that cheers you up." A case of poison ivy could have done a better job. No wonder the very next sentence after Eliphaz runs out of steam like the last stink bomb in the fireworks stand, is Job's reply:

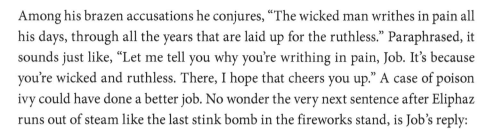

Miserable comforters are you all
(Job 16:2).

Eliphaz's words were windy (according to Job in 16:3), but notice how he tried to clout himself up by telling his age, along with the age of the rest of the nightmare counseling team. "Older than your father," he says, "the grey-haired and the aged" (15:10). I wish I could say it doesn't sound familiar. It's a minority, I hope, but sometimes the gray-haired and aged want you to know they're like Farmers Insurance. They know a thing or two because they've seen a thing or two.

Most of us laid aside coloring when we were five just after kindergarten, but one day five shows up again, and this time it's in the tens column, and suddenly coloring makes a huge comeback. We can't color the gray hairs fast enough before they sprout out again. It's like a hopeless game of whack-a-mole.

Some, like Eliphaz, think it means we've got all the answers. Well, the years are certainly a teacher. But it doesn't give us a right to jump to conclusions, like Eliphaz did. It doesn't mean that a few laugh lines and hot flashes have earned us the right, ever, to make a sister who feels bad, like Job (without the y chromosome part), feel worse. And if we learn anything from Eliphaz and company, it certainly doesn't make us right or her wrong. If Mama's pointing fingers at the one who's already down, get her off the wrecking ball!

What if Job's friends had used their years' experience to encourage Job? What if they had said, "God has always pulled me through, and he will pull you through as well"; "You're going to make it, Job; we're going to be here for you"?

There would have still been tears, pain, and suffering, but there would have been a joy in the relationship that Job would have remembered all his days. We can choose to be that kind of friend. All of us can, but especially those of us who can reach out to the younger ones and say, "I believe in you. I know you can do this. I've lived long enough to see just how big God is."

I remember someone once saying to me, "There are times when we can't see how it's ever even going to be possible to recover from something this hard and tragic, but God can do things that seem impossible to us." Back up to the first two words of that sentence you just read. I remember. I hung on to that hope like it was the last loaf of bread before an Alabama snow flurry. Our words, when they reflect God's truth and goodness, give people hope.

Build Up the One Who Is Sacrificing

Don't forget the woman in John 12 who brought a very expensive gift to Jesus. It was a sacrifice, and immediately, the criticism began. Why? Why does it always? There are a number of reasons, and we don't know them all, but I'd say at the forefront, Satan hates enthusiasm that explodes from giving our best to Jesus. There is a great joy that comes from sacrifice, and Satan wants to steal any true happiness from it and replace it with fake happiness. Satan's pearls are always fake, and sometimes even Christians will grab at them. I think it works like this. If I'm not sacrificing as much as I should, maybe my strand of pearls will look shinier if I dull yours a little. Whatever the rationale, those who are sacrificing the most sometimes get criticized the harshest.

Some among us strut around the sacrificial altar like we're the one who brought the lamb. Have you ever heard something like this? "I can't believe that family would up and become missionaries with two young children. What if they need a good doctor?" Or how about this? "Those people are going to put themselves in a financial bind the way they're sending all their kids off to a Christian college."

Let's get this straight. Whatever Christians are doing because their hearts are convicted that they ought to offer more than they have before, no matter how you feel personally about it, they are doing it as sacrifice to the Lord. This means the couple downsizing from Upper Oakwood Haven Heights to Lower Fit-It-All-in-a-Trailer so they can travel helping small congregations; it means the ones giving up a year of their lives to go to politically uncertain corners of the world to teach English using the Bible as the text; it means the ones giving up careers in order to teach their own children in an environment where the truth and scripture will permeate every subject in the curriculum. Whatever the sacrifice, it doesn't have to be what you would do in those shoes, but neither would I want to be in the shoes of the one criticizing. If Mama's honing in on someone else's sacrifice, get her off the wrecking ball.

Choose happiness over contempt! Be the person that says, "I appreciate your sacrifice. I want to be part of this; let me do something to help." Or at the very least, do what Jesus said to do in John 12, and "leave her alone."

> Jesus said, "Leave her alone, so that she may keep it for the day of my burial" (John 12:7).

Build Up Those Who Are Rejoicing

It seems that in the very best of days and circumstances, there is always that one. There is that one that mocks our celebration, and says, "You'll see." Don't be that one, and don't be mistaken about who's coaching your team if you are.

We enjoy great successes as the Lord's people because he is with us, just as we prayed he would be. Each victory is a defeat for the enemy, Satan, so be prepared; he won't take it sitting down.

He didn't take it sitting down at Mt. Carmel, which sounds like a scrumptious oversized sundae but is really the place where fire from heaven consumed Elijah's sacrifice even though it was both drenched and entrenched with water. It was such a magnanimous victory that 1 Kings 18:39 says "When all the people saw it, they fell on their faces and said, 'The Lord, he is God; the Lord, he is God.'" It resulted in all the wicked prophets of Baal being destroyed. Not only this, but what followed was a huge rain ending a desperate famine. All was going exceptionally well for God's people.

Turn one page in your Bible. Elijah is now lying exhausted under a broom tree, being chased by Jezebel, and wishing he was dead. Satan the killjoy got busy quick.

In the book of Jonah, after the fish upchucked (2:10), there was a success (and not just that one). Jonah's short sermon was so successful that one of the most wicked cities in ancient history had a change of heart (3:5). What a celebration this should have been.

Turn one page in your Bible. Jonah invited that killjoy to sit down beside him in the shade. Sad. Jonah didn't even need a third man. He just allowed Satan to talk him into criticizing God during the tremendous success.

In Joshua 6, the Israelites walked around a fortified wall of a major city the seventh time, the priests blew the trumpets, the people shouted, and the wall fell flat. Never has there been a more victorious military maneuver. In fact, the chapter ends like this: "So the Lord was with Joshua, and his fame was in all the land."

Satan the killjoy got busy quick.

Turn one page in your Bible. Satan apparently got up from his recliner. "But the people of Israel broke faith" (Josh. 7:1). Soon we find Joshua with his face to the ground crying "Why?"

In the Lord's church, some days are fire-from-heaven days. Oh, I know the age of miracles is over (1 Cor. 13), but the one who instigated them is alive and well, and we can see with certainty his blessing our efforts in his kingdom. Some days are upchucking whale days. We navigate through some unforeseen mess that may have been caused by our own lack of foresight. But somehow in rolling up our sleeves and confronting whatever it is that's upstaging the peace and calm right now, the Lord brings results greater than we could have ever planned on our own. At times we feel like we've been up against the same wall for days on end, but when we begin to feel completely exhausted and defeated, we see the wall begin to crumble just as we have earnestly prayed.

These are jubilant days. And the devil hates a Christian's jubilee. He gets up. First Chronicles 21:1 gives us this insight: "Then Satan stood against Israel." Many translations say he stood up; this coming right after Israel's slaughter of several giants. The more important the cause of rejoicing, the more he will use whatever means he can to ruin it.

Don't Be the Killjoy!

I don't say this to discourage you. This is a book about happiness, for crying out loud! If your congregation has had success, if your ladies' group has put heart and soul into an effort, if your young people have mastered another level of Bible knowledge, go ahead and rejoice. Rejoice big! God wants you to (Neh. 8:9–12; Luke 15:23; 1 Thess. 5:16), and if a lost soul has returned, it's a remarkably good day, and he's rejoicing himself (Luke 15:10).

But when Satan stands up, he's going to use the tool in close reach. Don't let it be you. How close to the success can a person be, and still be the catalyst for discouragement? Achan was among the wall-marchers. Jezebel had just seen the famine come to an end. Jonah couldn't have been closer to the situation—he's the title character. Sometimes the very killjoy comes from those who should be doing the cheering. While I may not be a thief like Achan or hopefully carry the weight in wickedness of Jezebel, can I be just as responsible for smoldering a flame of fervor? Truth be told, the religious pillars like Joshua and Elijah were a little responsible for a "woe is me; all is undone" spirit here.

Often our victories are followed by challenges.

Often our victories are followed by challenges, and that's okay; we'll suit up in Christian armor (Eph. 6:10–18) and God will carry us through. But sometimes our joy does not have to be train-wrecked. It's just that some among us choose to sabotage it. How?

I've been at gospel meetings that were so successful, people were having to get creative to make up parking spaces, and that was the focus for some. This influx of crowds to hear the gospel was nothing but a parking problem. I've sat in sermons that were so persuasive through scripture that one or two from the pews gave a hearty amen. And that became the focus. People were a little too enthused about the message, and it was just a little irritating to be woken up in the middle of church like that. I've seen people walk out during a baptism because it was cutting into their lunch. I've seen children reprimanded for getting up on their knees in the chair so they could better see the visuals of stories of Jesus.

Those were all moments for rejoicing, rejoicing, rejoicing! And they instead became triggers for tearing down, tearing down, tearing down. In times like these, Mama's on the wrecking ball. Or someone is. Get her off!

Build one another up instead, and be happy. Isn't that what 1 Thessalonians 5:11 says? Give people affirmation that all the work has paid off. Give God the glory constantly. Hug. Smile. Rejoice. Laugh. Encourage. Pray together. Give a thumbs-up to the little song leader as he passes you on the way back to his pew, his little heart racing.

> *Therefore encourage one another and build one another up, just as you are doing (1 Thess. 5:11).*

Build Up Those Who Are Working

Galatians 6:9 tells us not to grow weary in doing good. I do believe, in context, this is mainly talking about financial good. But surely its application is to every kind of good we can do. Paul's letter reminds us because it's way too easy to become exhausted, overwhelmed, or feel like "I'm the only one."

That's why hard workers need us to build them up, to give them stamina to complete the job. I believe the book of Nehemiah is one of the best work manuals in print. The whole purpose of Nehemiah's work team was to build up. They did it physically, but they also did it spiritually.

Nehemiah's first item on the agenda was prayer. Prayer makes the difference between solid building up and fluffy flattering. It's nice to hear "Good job," but I'd rather hear "I'm praying for you." I'd rather hear, "God's blessing us."

Nehemiah talked to the king, but not until he had already talked to *the* King, so that he started his project with, "And the king granted me what I asked, for the good hand of my God was upon me" (2:8). He had prayed for success (1:11), and he was certain of both the power of God and his place as a servant worker. "The God of heaven will make us prosper, and we his servants will arise and build" (2:20).

The work was well-prayed and well-organized. Around forty groups of workers are named in Nehemiah 3. I can just imagine the fun they were having. Oh, they were serious in purpose and diligence, but there's just something about God's people working hard that brings wheelbarrows and shovels full of laughter and happiness.

But here comes the wrecking ball. "Now when Sanballat heard that we were building the wall, he was angry and greatly enraged, and he jeered at the Jews" (Neh. 4:1). By chapter 6, Nehemiah had practically finished the wall except for the doors, when Sanballat and Geshem sent him a message to come down and meet with them. His answer was short and direct:

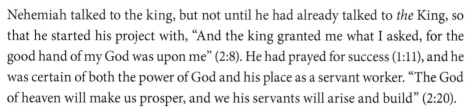

I am doing a great work and I cannot come down. Why should the work stop while I leave it and come down to you?
(Neh. 6:3).

Have you ever had to stop a work you were doing for the Lord when you were almost finished with it because someone didn't like the way you were doing it? They want us to stop until we can have a meeting about this. I remember once when my husband was in youth ministry, the youth group became quite enthusiastic about redoing their classroom, and they were scraping, scrubbing, and painting when they could have been home doing nothing at best, and out making trouble at worst. (It would break your hearts if I shared their upbringing.)

And at this point, you can just substitute another name for Sanballat in the verse I mentioned above. "Now when some of the longstanding members heard that we were painting the chairs, they were angry and greatly enraged." What a shame that we had to stop what we were doing to have a meeting—to make peace with the members without breaking the spirit of the teens.

On more than one occasion, I have received back-to-back emails, the first of which was brimming with excitement about the work that was being done for an upcoming ladies' day: what lessons they were planning, the scriptures that would go with them, the songs that would work best, and the follow-up planned for visitors. This was followed by a never-mind email. There had been a meeting, and it was decided that it was just too much to try to put something of that caliber together. Often, such enthusiasm is quelled by one person.

We need fewer meetings and more elbow grease.

We have also trained children in texts of the Bible, preparing them for a Bible Bowl. Through this method, they have learned more Bible than most adults know, including myself. This makes me happier than a seventy-five percent off sale on cheesecake. The children are doing so well, but then the adults step in, and they're just not so sure they like the competition aspect of it. Wait, you don't like what is working better than anything we've tried yet to permanently engrave Bible truths in their hearts? These are children! Competition is more than okay when it comes to seeing who can hit a ball the hardest, who can do their chores the fastest, and who can spell esquamulose. I think what eight out of ten of the criticizing adults are really saying is, wait! I didn't realize the Bible would take so much of our time.

I'm not saying meetings are a bad idea, and certainly, as was the case with Nehemiah, prayer and planning up front are critical components of any project, as is getting the backing and wisdom of the others (Neh. 2:17–18), especially the leadership. In all of the aforementioned instances that was done. But it's my opinion that we need fewer meetings and more elbow grease. We need more answers like Nehemiah's. Whatever the case, it's certain that when we're working the hardest, we don't need Mama riding in on a wrecking ball!

We need builder-uppers. Get a paintbrush, get a flip chart, put on your door-knocking shoes, and get to work. Notice, those who criticized the woman in John 12 were the ones standing around. They usually are.

Build Up Those Who Are Closest to Us

When we stand a hundred yards back with a water hose, or as we say in the South, hosepipe, we may be able, with a good aim, to lightly mist someone. But when we move to within one foot of the person, we can completely drench her. Influence is like that. The closer we are to a person, the more likely we can drench her with our influence. Make sure it's the right kind.

When David was so confident God could kill a giant that he was absolutely brave enough to step up to Goliath's challenge, the one who could have been the most encouraging to him proved to be the opposite.

> Now Eliab his eldest brother heard when he spoke to the men. And Eliab's anger was kindled against David, and he said, "Why have you come down? And with whom have you left those few sheep in the wilderness? I know your presumption and the evil of your heart, for you have come down to see the battle" (1 Sam. 17:28).

Not one lady reading this book will ever be an older brother, but a hundred percent of them will be an older sister at some point. Even if you're a teen or a tween, you're older than someone. Those younger sisters in your congregation need you to build them up as they gain the confidence to get involved in more good works and studies.

Not only the spiritual family is germane to this discussion, but also the physical one. David's flesh-and-blood brother could have been a great encouragement to him. Ladies, our husbands and children can benefit more from our encouragement than those who stand a hundred feet away. Moms, it's easy for us to be involved in so many good works that we forget the best one. Let's make sure we're encouraging our children, motivating them to greater service and Bible knowledge. It means we love crayon-produced drawings given to widows more than we love hanging Rembrandts in the church foyer. It means we have more time to sit down and drill the Bible questions than we have to make the chicken salad for the ladies' day. It means we say, "I know you can do it," when your child wonders if he could ever write a bulletin article or teach a lesson, and you hand him a pen and paper to get started.

Building up means you say, "This is a wonderful sacrifice of your time," more than you say, "Quit wasting my time." You say, "Well done, good and faithful servant," because you want, more than anything in the world, for your child to hear those words on judgment day.

Remember, a child is not going to produce adult work. He feels a risk when he does something new, whether it's raking a yard or standing up in front of a group of adults to give his first lesson. Our goal is to mold and shape his heart Godward. It is not to tear down all the effort he has put forth. There is a place for constructive criticism, but it should never be on the child's first attempt, and it should always follow, "Here's what I loved about what you did." In fact, when listening or watching, that's what we should be looking for—what was good. We then can follow (assuming this is not every time) with how she could make it even better, with words like, "I just bet you could do that!"

Mold and shape his heart Godward.

If nothing else comes from this chapter, let's take one thing home. Our reaction to another person's work can be completely pivotal. It can cause a person to say, "I give up," or to say, "Well, I didn't do too bad; I think I'll try again." In that way, our building up can literally make the difference in all of eternity for a soul you can't put a price on. Get off the wrecking ball and on the construction site.

It took days to build up the fireworks stand mentioned at the beginning of this chapter, but only a minute or two for the entire destruction of it. It can take a lifetime of little shots of encouragement to build up a person into what she can be for the Lord. But in a moment, one fiery tongue can tear down all hope of her wanting to try again.

Think about it. You're a firecracker. Do your job, but don't blow up the whole place!

> *So also the tongue is a small member, yet it boasts of great things. How great a forest is set ablaze by such a small fire! (James 3:5).*

If You're Happy, You Will Know It

1. Consider this sentence: "Get a paintbrush, get a flip chart, put on your door-knocking shoes, get to work." What other items would you add to that list? Where, as women, can we jump in and make an eternal difference with our work?

2. What do you think of the hosepipe principle—the closer we are, the greater the influence? If this is true, what are some specific ways that we, first, can get closer to a person?

3. The Bible doesn't really tell us what happened to David and Eliab's relationship in 1 Samuel 17. Knowing how this story unfolded, what do you think is likely to have developed between them?

4. While it's true that we have a greater influence over those closest to us, do you believe we also have a greater propensity to hurt those closest to us? What about to forgive those closest to us?

5. What do we learn about influence from the mothers of the kings as they are often briefly mentioned in 1 and 2 Kings and 1 and 2 Chronicles? What usually follows the mention of a mother's name in these accounts?

6. No matter how old you are, get some mommy-and-me time with your daughter, son, or your mother this week. Plan a specific work that you are going to do together for the sake of Christ. It can be a benevolent work for another Christian, a bulletin board, a social media ladies' broadcast—anything worthwhile for the kingdom! At the end of it all, send an encouraging note in the mail to your kid or parent, thanking her and pointing out the

strengths she gave to the project and the fun you had, even if she lives in the same house with you.

7. Nehemiah took some extensive time to pray, evaluate, and plan before he began his work. What are the necessary steps to take before you begin a ladies' work?

8. Make a list of the ten people who are younger than you over which you think you can have the greatest influence. Circle the person you can encourage right now, and do it!

Happy Trails

And speaking of fireworks . . .

Now, what's the point exactly again? You spend a lot of money, and then destroy the items you just bought on purpose? How did this idea ever get through *Shark Tank*?

"Yes, I have a business proposal. You sell people things made out of paper and gunpowder, and then they self-destruct the first time they're used."

"Okay, but if you do it more than two times a year, the average consumer will catch on to the scheme."

So they got with the people who make the American calendar, and set aside two days for exploding things every year. These are July 4 and December 31.

This resulted in trailers popping up everywhere which say in huge misspelled letters, CHEEPEST FARWORKS ANYWHEAR. Cheapest is a word that comes from the same Latin root for the word *bankrupt*. These trailers are up for a solid six weeks prior to explosion day, commonly offering "buy one, get one free" packages. This is so you can lose the hearing in both ears at the same time, but only pay for one.

Now, there is apparently a law in some states that proprietors can set up the sale of self-destructing goods outside of the six-week period, as in all the time, in permanently fixed buildings as long as they are within a spit and a stick's throw of a major interstate, and provided they have letters the size of Godzilla that say "World's Largest Fireworks Stand." Oh yeah, and they must say, "Last Chance." Last chance for what? Is this the last chance I will have to blow up? Is this the last chance to spend my inheritance? What is it? I have to know.

Whatever it is, it's enough pressure to cause my father to blow the inheritance (no pun intended). This is the man who was so cheap, he refused to pay the exorbitant amount of $7.50 per month for garbage pick-up because that translated to an outrageous $1.87 per week. He despised throwing money away by allowing the tiniest soap shard to be dispensed with, and instead gathered all the little pieces until he had enough to melt them back together into a "new" soap cake.

And yet—and *yet*—when these two days of the year rolled around, he threw money out the window like he was Howard Hughes at a spend-off. When he became too frail to drive to the fireworks stand, he sent a young, trusted friend, Grat, who assisted him with those kind of challenges, to purchase the fireworks. He assured him he would reimburse him for whatever the amount was, but instructed him to buy a big variety. Grat was somewhat nervous about showing him the bill because it didn't take long to drive the amount up to $257. Dad's jaws dropped open, and he said, "I can't believe it; that's a lot less than I spent last year." Relief. Followed by a slight concern that an alien had inhabited my dad's body.

But no real invasion. It's just part of the show. The show that one year escalated to hysteria and near-death experiences. We had gathered in Dad's back yard as was the tradition. A couple of the guys in the family were in charge of the lighting-the-fuses part, but I don't believe they had ever graduated from Smokey the Bear's safety course. This is where the grand finale was grander than anyone could have imagined. Just before the intertwined fuses of every breed of explosive known to man or chemistry lab reached the gunpowder, the entire pack fell over on its side facing the helpless crowd of us. We were running for cover and hitting the concrete like Al Capone had appeared with a machine assault rifle. My brother became a human bullet-proof vest for my father who could neither dive nor dash at this point. I thought it would never end. My nephew was strutting around like James Bond after the ordeal because his wedding band had deflected a missile. And my sister, who wouldn't answer our calls, and who we thought must surely be wounded beyond response, had missed the whole thing on a quick trip to the bathroom.

Not everyone can have a show so grand. Truthfully, we have struggled to recreate the festivities now that Dad has passed away. My brother-in-law and nephew staged a fireworks show this past New Year's Eve. The wind worked against them, the products were substandard, so that half of them fizzled instead of exploding, and the sky lantern did little more than skip along the lawn.

Rather than disappoint the children, the sister who previously had escaped the war zone show, now redeemed herself by saving the sleepy one. She lit a couple of sparklers and took center stage twirling them in the dark as if she were suddenly competing for the poster girl for High School Majorettes Anonymous. I truly think she pulled a groin muscle, but we were all delighted and could probably have sold enough tickets, had we known, to pay for a new truck for the Volunteer Fire Department which, you know, we seem to need on two conspicuous days of the year.

When all is said and obliterated, there's just something fun about blowing things up. Unless you're under four. Or you're a dog. These two classes of individuals are completely terrorized. We try to console the little ones by holding them tight in a blanket and cupping our hands over their ears. The dogs prove to be a little more of a challenge, as their fight or flight instinct is pronounced.

Unfortunately at camp one year, the annual stray showed up for love and affection, but on the night of the fireworks show, we found out he was definitely inclined to fight over flight. He had watched in terror as the bottle rockets exploded in the sky until, finally, he'd had enough. As the cost-more-than-college-tuition finale was lit, he gulped big and made the move of his lifetime. He darted toward the enemy military, for the sake of all his beloved campers, tackled it headlong, and heroically backflipped into the lake with it where it expired pathetically with a little splash of a eulogy.

I haven't even touched on the great fire of 2006 or the two-hour fireworks birthday bash in which not even one fuse would cooperate to stay lit in the Delta winds or someone's great idea to have a fireworks show on a barge—I mean, what could happen, right? There's water all around.

Famous last words. Next significant semi-annual event, can we skip a step, and just go ahead and set fire to the back yard?

IF MAMA AIN'T HAPPY,
Quitters Never Are
Defeat or Determination

Who put this schedule together? Not someone with four kids. All of ours were playing ball on the same Saturday. We thought, when we signed up on the family plan, we were getting a bargain. It turns out that we were trading our sanity for a few sunburns and a lot of near cardiac emergencies running between fields. I actually had to hire someone in the youth group to watch one of my kids play because there just weren't enough parents to go around.

Enoch was almost five. He should have been home feeding Cheerios into the air vents like every other kid of mine at his age. But he was spruced up in a bright uniform advertising a local bank. At least he didn't get on the bail bonding team. I promise it existed.

He was all about that number on his jersey and his ball cap, and all I heard was "When's my ballgame?" from Sunday to Saturday. This is the league where one parent has to stand in the field next to the child to tell him all the ways not to run and all the things not to do with the ball. It is never successful.

How did I always end up being the out-on-the-field parent while the other parent got the sitting-in-the-shade watching a real game between ten-year-olds job? So Enoch and I would stand there, and he'd jump up and down and hit home runs because of egregious errors by the other team. He'd throw the ball halfway to first, he'd occasionally tag someone out, and he only hit an adult with a bat a couple of times. It was great fun. For one inning. They played two at that age.

Every Saturday, at exactly the time the second inning started, Enoch was done in his soul. He was a quitter with no shame about it. His only thought was a purple slushie from the concession stand which he called a kickstand. It's a good thing there was dirt to draw in and an occasional helicopter overhead or I believe he would have died right there from boredom, slowly sinking into despair.

He was four. Most everyone reading this has surpassed that age by at least a decade or two. Most of us have committed our lives to Christ, and more than a few of us could hear an auditorium full of people dragging a chorus of "No turning back; no turning back" while we were throwing our dripping baptismal garments into a laundry bin. If that's the case, we've all also met the enemy unexpectedly when we were rounding a corner or topping a hill. We've had hard days and trying nights. We've been disappointed and road-blocked. But we're not four anymore. We can't just quit after the first inning.

The Beginning Inning

There is no greater feeling than the one when you're wringing wet from baptism. Everything that was wrong with your soul's condition and forecast is suddenly right. You're God's now. His grace is big enough to erase your most sordid sin, and you feel an enthusiasm that can take on the world.

Well, get ready because you're about to! I struggle with whether to say anything about this. I don't want to focus on negative things that can come our way at a time we should bask in the joy of forgiveness. But to maintain a positive perspective, we've got to be proactive rather than reactive. Football teams don't get pep talks in the locker room because there is nothing out there but fluffy cotton balls in pretty pastel colors being carried by soft, furry bunny rabbits. There's a team out there that wants to take you down! Now get excited enough about what's at stake to overcome! No quitters allowed.

Satan Wants You Back

You see, you weren't really the focus of Satan's tactics before you became a Christian. He already had you. As long as you had sins that were not washed away, no matter how big or little by man's standards, he was good with it. You were already his.

Oh but now, now you've become a very interesting project. He intends to get you back. And the deal is, you're more of a prize now because if he gets you, he will invariably get others because of you.

Do you teach a Bible class? He'd love to have you because look at all the little souls that would be hurt if you gave up now. Why work on each one of them when he could take you instead, and get them all with one blow?

Don't Be Satan's Target

A word here to wives: Satan's working on your husband, but he also knows a shortcut. If he can discourage you, you'll most likely take care of the rest. It's true in most marriages, but exponentially in church leaders' families. If the woman wants to quit, the husband can only stagger along unsupported carrying a huge burden for so long before collapsing or laying it aside.

Moms, do I even have to go here? It's so obvious that you're a favorite target for Satan. If Mom gets disinterested in the Lord's work, if Mom gets lazy with Bible study and feels defeated by the pressures pulling her in every direction, if Mom is fatigued to the point of quitting, Satan will almost assuredly get the children.

That's a sonic boom alarm by the way. This is your cue for the line: "*My* children? Over my dead body!" This is where determination wins over defeat. This is where you say, "I will not quit."

But how?

Hebrews 11 is a favorite chapter for most of us. It puts all our Bible flip charts in one place. There's Enoch, walking with God. There's Abel, offering a more excellent sacrifice than Cain. There's Rahab; hiding the spies. All the greats are there, but what's the point? In two words, don't quit!

The discussion really starts in the chapter before. Look at Hebrews 10:19–22.

> Therefore, brothers, since we have confidence to enter the holy places by the blood of Jesus, by the new and living way that he opened for us through the curtain, that is, through his flesh, and since we have a great high priest over the house of God, let us draw near with a true heart in full assurance of faith, with our hearts sprinkled clean from an evil conscience and our bodies washed with pure water.

Remember, Draw Near, Remove Obstacles, Enjoy Access

"Don't quit" shoulders every sentence. First of all, don't forget the incredible significance of your baptism. That one event removed the sin that was standing between you and God. We can draw near now. Grasp the meaning. If something such as a huge vase of gladiolas, is in the way of the person we're trying to talk to at the dinner table, we remove it.

Baptism removes sin. It was the thing in the way between you and the one you need to have a lifelong conversation with. There is nothing between you and God now. You are right there. Anything preventing you from access has been removed. You belong.

We don't sneak in a back door to get a glimpse of God. We enter his presence with all the boldness of a daughter who marches right through the kitchen door of her parents' home without knocking. We have full access. We never outgrow that in the physical realm. My father never once said, "What are you doing in this house? Why don't you knock?" He never expected me to ask before going to the refrigerator or the bathroom. I had full access to everything without thinking about anything. He was my father.

Stir, Don't Separate!

Emerging from that realization, there's a responsibility to stir the pot. The good one. If we're going to hang on and hang in, we need each other.

> *And let us consider how to stir up one another to love and good works (Heb. 10:24).*

Our relationship with other Christians is mutually dependent. We stir them up, and doing it, we strengthen ourselves.

There's a ridiculous instruction in most recipes that says, "Separate the eggs." After wasting a few years and a few hundred eggs trying to do this the old fashioned way, enter Pinterest. I didn't realize that I and every woman that ever walked into a kitchen, be it colonial or mid-century modern, had been doing most of life wrong until Pinterest. Before that time, we had taken "separate the eggs" to mean:

1. Try to crack them on the edge of a bowl.

2. Try to crack them on the edge of the counter.

3. Try to crack them on the cast iron skillet.

4. Get a towel and repeat steps 1–3.

5. When you have successfully cracked the egg, try to pour out the white part without pouring out the little round ball.

6. After several attempts, you will have a long string of gooey stuff that won't pull away from the broken egg shell.

7. Twist the egg shell around to a sharp point and try to cut the goo away.

8. Puncture the yolk by mistake. Repeat steps 1–6.

Then, after literally thousands of years of women doing this in the kitchen—I mean, truth be told, this is probably why Martha came running out into the den blaming her sister for not helping her; I just bet her hands were a little yellow with egg yolk—finally, Pinterest tells us (with pictures and video), all you have to do is pour the egg in the bowl, squeeze an empty water bottle, and then vacuum the yolk up into the bottle. It's that easy.

In case you wonder what application I can possibly make here, it's this. We can easily be sucked up from our newfound life in Christ. I think the parable of the sower makes that point (Matt. 13:19).

But if, before I get that water bottle vacuum, I beat that egg—I stir it up—there is no water bottle on the planet that can separate the yolk from the white. It can't be done.

Sisters, stir one another up! Get all up in each other's lives. It's difficult, if not impossible, for the enemy to pull us away from the church when we continue to make ourselves inseparable by the stirring of our lives together.

If Mama Ain't Happy, Is She Missing This?

Now get the rest. It all flows right into Hebrews 10:25, the assembly. Don't miss it. Not once. The Hebrews writer talks about the encouragement we receive, but what else? Oh, "so much more" are almost the exact words. "Not neglecting to meet together, as is the habit of some, but encouraging one another, and all the more as you see the Day drawing near." It's a "don't quit" pep talk. There's a finish line; we see the Day drawing near. There are some who are in the habit of missing, and if Mama ain't happy, she might be one of them. We get the encouragement there to last the week. It's spiritual grocery shopping. What if you don't get the groceries to last a week? Somebody's not going to be happy; somebody's going to be hungry. Go two weeks and starvation is imminent, leading quickly to death.

Whether it's a symptom or part of the problem—either way a break in attendance is a shortcut to the q-word. It's rare that people totally quit the church and forfeit salvation, though they may experience internal struggles, when they are faithfully joining in assembly. On the other hand, there is a sure break-up with the first love (Rev. 2:4) if a Christian quits assembling.

We understand it in every other realm of life. Imagine considering yourself part of a sports team if you never show up for the games. Even when players are injured, they show up, dress in the uniform, and sit on the bench. Even if life has hit us so hard we feel inadequate to teach, or we are so overwhelmed we can hardly turn the pages of the Bible, and our voice fails in song, we need to sit on the bench; we need to be with the team like never before.

Fearful Expectation

Don't quit. Your baptism was too significant. Your relationships are too important. Your assembling with the church is too valuable. But if that isn't enough, the next verses pull all the stops. We ought to be just plain afraid to quit. Listen! "For if we go on sinning deliberately after receiving the knowledge of the truth, there no longer remains a sacrifice for sins, but a fearful expectation of judgment, and a fury of fire that will consume the adversaries" (Heb. 10:26–27). That's not a popular approach. It's a good thing the Holy Spirit isn't interested in getting a People's Choice Award with his writing. He's interested in my soul.

Also, understand that because of the high price Christ paid for our salvation, God takes it very personally when we choose to forgo the prize. Rejecting Mosaic law was one thing, a bad thing with bad results: "Anyone who has set aside the law of Moses dies without mercy on the evidence of two or three witnesses" (Heb. 10:28), but quitting Christ is unconscionable, describing the person as one "who has trampled the Son of God underfoot, counted the blood of the covenant by which he was sanctified a common thing, and insulted the Spirit of grace" (v. 29). After quoting two scriptures from the Old Testament in verse 30 concerning the Lord's vengeance and his judgment, the writer punctuates the paragraph with the bottom line:

It's a "don't quit" pep talk.

> *It is a fearful thing to fall into the*
> *hands of the living God*
> *(Heb. 10:31).*

Take your pulse. You might be discouraged, but don't quit. Because after all, look how far you've come. You've been here before. The enemy's reared his ugly head a time or two in the past, and you're the one who not only conquered through Christ but also showed compassion to others in the struggle (Heb. 10:32–34). Realize that you've been an influence to others. Don't throw it away! "Therefore do not throw away your confidence, which has a great reward" (v. 35).

Don't Be a Shrinky Dink

Have I lost my mind? I'm ranting like I'm talking to a bunch of reprobates ready to jump ship at any moment into the Lost Sea, and not the one in Sweetwater, Tennessee. Most likely, if you're reading the ninth chapter of a spiritual study, you're not about to take the plunge. Exactly! The devil is crafty, persistent, but quitters are not who we are.

I love the last verse of the chapter with all my being: "But we are not of those who shrink back and are destroyed, but of those who have faith and preserve their souls" (Heb. 10:39).

We are not of those who shrink back.

Maybe you got one of those kits for Christmas a few decades ago. The ones where you color the plastic flowers and butterflies, and then you put them in the oven, and they shrink to tiny, pretty, but totally useless—um, things. Well, guess what? You're not them. You're not a Shrinky Dink. We are not of those who shrink back. Oh, we do the oven part. Remember 1 Peter 1:7? We go through the fire. It's painful, it's grueling at times, but we come out as fine gold, not useless plastic.

The Fiber of the Faithful

So there. That's Hebrews 10, and it goes right into the famous chapter 11 where we learn what faith is and who the faithful are. We'd love to be one of these spiritual giants, but let me ask you, which one of them do you want to trade places with first? Would you like to be the woman who had to "up and move" just when she was ready for social security, and no one told her where she was going, only that it was far? How about being pregnant when you're ninety? Sarah not only needed the book *What to Expect When You're Expecting*, I think she could have used a copy of *What to Do When You Weren't Expecting to Be Expecting at 90*. What were her cravings, Prevagen and a pickle? And don't forget, she had some family struggles the tabloids would have liked to have gotten wind of.

Would you like to trade places with the one holding a knife over his own son who is tied up? Would you like to send your other son away because your wife can't stand to look at him? Abraham did both.

Would you like to be sold as a slave? Left in a dark pit? Serve a prison sentence? All three? That's just a sliver of Joseph's trouble. And we haven't begun to dig into the depths of the heartaches of these and others in this Hall of Faith chapter.

If we read Hebrews 11, and really think about the personal struggles of each one listed, and if we had the chance to trade our circumstances for theirs, I think we'd say, "You know what? I think I'm good."

So what do we get from this list of Bible heroes? We're pretty sure it's about faith; that much is clear since it's repeated fourteen times in the chapter. But it's about the fiber of the faith—it's not just a pretty word written in cursive over a flower on a Bible cover. It endures the worst through the darkest. Somehow, this Hebrews 11 crew, as imperfect as they were, kept forging through threats down their backs, hungry lions, and heated furnaces. How? By faith.

How do we keep going when the tempest is raging within our walls, sin has tricked those dearest to us, or financial devastation throws us a surprise party? The same way. We know what they knew, by faith. They kept pressing on because they weren't trying to get to Wall Street or Pennsylvania Avenue or even past tax day. They were going to heaven, and they could see the substance of things hoped for.

Here's the deal. They had a promise of a Messiah, but we're on the other side of that promise. "And all these, though commended through their faith, did not receive what was promised, since God had provided something better for us, that apart from us they should not be made perfect" (Heb. 11:39–40).

All that they were seeking was wrapped up in what we have—who we have, Jesus our Savior. "These all died in faith, not having received the things promised, but having seen them and greeted them from afar, and having acknowledged that they were strangers and exiles on the earth" (Heb. 11:13). If they didn't quit seeing the promise afar off, I believe we ought to press on a little further. So does the Hebrews writer. Begin chapter 12.

Look at the Cloud!

My mother and grandmother used to step out onto the front porch when a storm was approaching just about the time a little darkness was cast on the lawn, the trees began to bow, and Mama and Dunca's dresses began to take on a life of their own. You could predict the words before they came out, "Whoo-oo, look at the cloud!"

When I finish Hebrews 11 and see that first verse of 12, those words come to mind. Whoo-oo, look at the cloud!

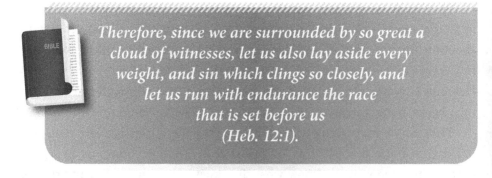

Therefore, since we are surrounded by so great a cloud of witnesses, let us also lay aside every weight, and sin which clings so closely, and let us run with endurance the race that is set before us (Heb. 12:1).

If a cloud this tremendous surrounds us, we've got to keep going, but not with that sin in tow. You know the one. Yes, that one—the one that clings so closely. The New American Standard Bible says it "easily entangles us."

Prepare to Be Entangled

I remember as a child, every time there was a promise of a light breeze, we tried to get a kite up when we were at the grandparents' house. They lived close to the National Guard Armory, whose practice field made a great open place to experiment with a homemade kite without the threat of a Charlie Brown wreck in a tree or a power line. One morning, we got out of bed and headed for our favorite spot dragging our (kite) tails behind us, and we were bummed that the soldiers were infringing on our kite plans with some ridiculous military maneuvers.

We headed back toward home mumbling something about "some nerve," but we didn't give up that easily. We ended up trying to fly the kite at the top of a little-traveled street. And wouldn't you know it. A whole platoon had left the armory and was marching the streets. They were focused, stiff, and doing all the hup, two, three things. We got pretty pulled in, and in watching the soldiers, my sister kind of forgot about the kite in the sky which she held the other end to in her hand. And when you forget about kites, they take a dive. And when they take a dive, you end up with a lot of string on the ground. And when you start reeling the string back in, stiff, marching soldiers get easily entangled.

> **Keep going, but not with that sin in tow.**

What? They are soldiers! They have a purpose much greater and nobler than worthless string. But they weren't expecting it. They weren't watching out for it, and they got entangled. It was really quite hilarious to us, but they didn't think so. Here you had grown, brawny men who were just recently a solid unit, so deeply regimented, they would rival Big Ben. Now they were bent over bumping into each other, losing their balance, pulling dime store thread from around their ankles. They were a mess.

It's like that sin that easily entangles us. We're spiritual soldiers. We are marching for a cause far greater than any nation or patriot ever did, but it seems like it gets us every time. It shows up when we're off guard, and there we are, pulled away from our cause to untangle the damage. What a mess!

Watch! Be ready for it! Whatever the temptation is, pray about it and immerse yourself in scripture. Why? Because, even for Jesus, these were the ultimate temptation weapons (Mark 4, Ephesians 6).

Stay as far away from temptation as you can. It entangles, but it also weights your stride to cripple your run. Lay it aside, and stay busy with better things. Run the race, because if you're not running, you'll pick it up again. But rarely—okay, let's go ahead and say never—never have I seen someone running in a race who stopped to pick up something before sprinting to the finish line.

Focus on the Finisher

And about that finish line, continue to Hebrews 12:2. "Looking to Jesus, the founder and perfecter of our faith, who for the joy that was set before him endured the cross, despising the shame, and is seated at the right hand of the throne of God."

If you want to cross the finish line, look to the finisher. If you're thinking this Christianity thing may be a little tougher than you can take, look to the one who bore it all. And if you need a little help getting up with the right attitude some mornings, understand that the innocent one who suffered unthinkable shame and cruel pain on my behalf did it with an attitude of . . . joy. He did what he utterly despised, what he asked if there was another way to accomplish (Matt. 26:39, 42), and what he dreaded with the kind of dread that produced huge sweat beads like drops of blood (Luke 22:44), only because he could see the joy that resulted on the other side of it.

I know that this joy included being restored to a heavenly dwelling and reigning with the Father, but that wasn't the totality of the joy. The joy that resulted was my joy. From the beginning, God's joy was that my destiny was changed. Hallelujah for a happiness not even on the same plane with any other! The joy that was set before him.

He endured incomprehensible suffering because of that finish line. What a shame if I quit this side of it! We've had days we've been through a grueling ringer, but we haven't done the Calvary kind of suffering, not yet, at least. The Hebrews writer said to those first century Christians, who suffered cruelty unknown by twenty-first century ones,

> *In your struggle against sin you have not yet resisted to the point of shedding your blood (Heb. 12:4).*

Take Your Whipping

Furthermore, get the lesson that these tests are good for you. In Alabama, we might say it this way: A little bit of whipping today will save you a whole lot of heartache tomorrow. It's not so far from these ancient words in this chapter:

> It is for discipline that you have to endure. God is treating you as sons. For what son is there whom his father does not discipline? If you are left without discipline, in which all have participated, then you are illegitimate children and not sons. Besides this, we have had earthly fathers who disciplined us and we respected them. Shall we not much more be subject to the Father of spirits and live? For they disciplined us for a short time as it seemed best to them, but he disciplines us for our good, that we may share his holiness. For the moment all discipline seems painful rather than pleasant, but later it yields the peaceful fruit of righteousness to those who have been trained by it (Heb. 12:7–11).

It doesn't need a lot of commentary, does it? In my raising, the women did the discipline mostly. I remember being frightened once of what most people call a daddy-long-legs spider, but in Alabama, we called them granddaddy spiders. My mother consoled me and said, "That's a granddaddy spider; granddaddies won't hurt you."

"No," I agreed. "But grandmothers sure will."

My daddy did spank me once, and it was just as the Hebrews writer said. It seemed best to him. Mama had called me in for supper, but I was too busy as there were many pretend rescues to make and errands to run on my tricycle in the driveway. It got a little darker, and they called me again. I still failed to respond. Soon, I had increased my route from the driveway to the street, and very soon my daddy removed me from my vehicle and administered the discipline.

Whether it's with a wooden spoon or, in my case, a hickory switch, this kind of love doesn't feel the greatest, but with good parents and not abusive ones, it was done with the greatest intention. Intention for our well-being, our future—to make us better and keep us on a safe path. If faulted humans who love imperfectly can impact our lives with consistent discipline, imagine what Almighty God, who loves us perfectly, can do through these trials for our eternal well-being.

You Better!

We call Hebrews a book about "better." In chapter 12, it becomes a book about "You better!" You better put that sin aside, you better look to Jesus, you better realize what you haven't suffered, and you better understand the benefit of what you have suffered. But hold on; don't leave the locker room yet until you've heard the next verse: "Therefore lift your drooping hands and strengthen your weak knees" (Heb. 12:12).

What a summation! Stand up straight, Mama! Don't let this life get to you, or you might miss the next one. Drooping hands and weak knees don't fortify lives, but busy hands and worn knees do.

True happiness, the joy kind, doesn't happen unless we're willing to endure through the trials and pain. Don't quit after the first inning. You're not four.

 **If You're Happy, You Will Know It**

1. In those tiny little league games, when the children want to quit, the parent is right there telling the child he can make it. How does that parallel Hebrews chapters 10, 11, and 12?

2. Is it true that if you decide every day when you get up, I will not quit today, then you will never quit? I have found, just in recent years, that if I write down, in the morning, how I will live today and why, my resolve is strengthened for that day. Try this for a week and reflect on its value at the end of the week. If it has helped your walk, continue this every morning from now on.

3. If you have never separated a yolk from a white with the empty water bottle method, try it. (If you need a reason, you can make me a cake.) Now, write down three parallels of this object lesson to Satan's craftiness.

4. Have you ever seen sporadic attendance to a secular activity affect the person's success in it? What was the activity and what was the result?

Happy Trails

And speaking of dripping baptismal garments . . .

It's the only thing more important than fifth Sunday singings, this side of heaven. It is who we are and what we are about. We know that without it, man stands in a lost and hopeless condition. It is God's generous offer to erase a miserable past, level us on even ground with one another, and above all else, give us access to his marvelous grace and our eternal salvation. It all takes place as he designed, in what someone way back nicknamed, "the watery grave of baptism."

There is no question—it's paramount. We know that as surely as the church was established in Acts 2, the Christian conversions that follow all have one integral and obvious denominator—baptism. But to look at the design of our buildings, you wouldn't think so.

I have moved all over the Southeast and been on evangelistic campaigns in four countries, and I am left dumbfounded by one haunting question: Who designed these things, and is it possible that he worked for the enemy? Entirely.

Or is it just that any doubts about the individual's sincerity or commitment are completely relinquished by his willingness to go through with this once he sees the mechanics?

It generally starts like this—a sequel to a Hitchcock movie. We introduce the enthusiastic prospect to our building through archways and stained glass and elaborate light fixtures, past padded pews to the side of a carpeted stage where a too-little-used door awaits. We jump two or three times to knock the key off the nail above the door.

As soon as the key is turned, we transition from imitation Baroque to bona fide broke. Chipped tile is exposed by the one seven-watt bare bulb above, but it soon gives way to a long set of incredibly steep, wooden stairs.

Convicted by the Word, we begin the ascent in single file (of necessity) only to find that two out of three times, the deacon over building and grounds has drained the thing at the precise moment you actually needed it! This has led, on more than one occasion, to singing all the stanzas of the first thirty songs in the songbook with the soft background accompaniment of the hosepipe running over fiberglass. It has been known to have providential results in which the extra time has worked on the hearts and minds of others present, turning one baptism into half a dozen. In those cases, it was well worth the inconvenience, but consider the other times—when the stateside missionary and his wife, having the vocal range of a Weedeater, alone are stalling for time by singing all four parts to the complete works of *Christian Hymns III* in front of a person who, up to this time, has never heard a gospel song that wasn't sung by Elvis.

That's the worst scenario, followed by a close second. The baptistry is full of clean water in this case, but this time someone has made a private decision of his own. Why spend fortunes of the Lord's money to heat hundreds of gallons of water all week, when it is only needed for a few minutes' time? I recently met my husband at the building after his studying with a young family. It was late, way past their kids' bedtimes, but they bundled them in coats and caps and blankets and braved the unusually bitter cold that night.

We immediately turned on the heat in the building, but it was going to take more than that. After all, they were going to shortly be soaking wet, and huge rooms with vaulted ceilings don't lend themselves to being heated quickly. We gathered up a few space heaters to place in the changing rooms, only to discover—get this!—there were no outlets in the baptistry area. Not one.

There are enough outlets in that building to light a large city. Someone tell me: What is the thinking behind a design like this? What would that have been, an extra four dollars in the building budget? I guess there's no need in putting an outlet at the top of a stairway that's too narrow to get a vacuum cleaner up, and no carpet anyway. We ended up threading a long, orange extension cord above the water and halfway down the auditorium aisle to an outlet. How safe is that?

It didn't help that there was a language barrier between us and our new brother and sister whom we love so dearly. But there was one Spanish word I learned that night: *frio,* which I think means, "My towel is frozen to my karate outfit."

Which brings me to another amazing design concept I'd like to discuss. These karate outfits, these baptismal garments if you will. Is there anyone alive reading this who can tell me how to put these on? We usually end up doing it like this: "Well, let's see, this part I guess wraps around under this, and pull it through this hole."

"That's the armhole."

"Right, but if this goes here, where's the other armhole?"

"Oh, I get it. Pull this up around your waist."

"But that leaves this hanging down."

I suddenly see why it takes so many people to go back there with the person being baptized.

The person baptizing, on the other hand, gets to wear something that looks like it's off the cover of "Field and Stream." I always thought the idea of the waders was to keep water out, but the first ten years my husband baptized people, he used them to bail water in. I always wondered why the preacher holds his hand up at a baptism. Maybe it's because John the Baptist does it in that picture in the Bible. But I think it has more to do with hoisting up that suspender to avoid waterlog.

Still, it is the best moment in life. A "new creature" comes forth from the water as pure as a baby. All the sins are erased. The slate is clean. If God could just take us at that moment, before the world gets its choke on us again, before temptation rears its pestering head and beats at the door. As the new Christian turns to descend that same steep stairwell, only wet this time, we are frightfully reminded that it could be entirely possible.

I must admit, I've been in the baptistry a few more times than I've meant to. This is because of the unfortunate placement of these things. Most of the time, they are right behind the stage. Good so far. You can usually step into the baptistry from the right or from the left. Good so far. However, there is usually no possible way to get around the baptistry without going through the watery grave. If a ledge exists on the front or the back, it is millimeters at best, so that if you wish to hang something sensible over that wall, such as a huge stuffed lion for VBS, you end up taking tiny ballerina steps around the edge with hammer and fishing line in one hand and Leo in the other, and we can surely all imagine the outcome of that.

Don't tell me I'm the only one.

Originally published in Christian Woman *magazine, September/October 2009.*

10

IF MAMA AIN'T HAPPY,
She Ate the Wrong Biscuit

Having to or Wanting To?

You can get money just for being cute. It used to happen to my kids all the time. A complete stranger would reach in his pocket, open his wallet, and for no reason at all, hand one of my children a dollar. They would imagine all the things they would buy with it, as if they had just inherited the Gates' fortune. I remember one Saturday, Enoch came running up to us with a crisp dollar bill. He was particularly enthralled with it as he turned it over a few times and held it up to the light. He smiled big, and said, "I'm gonna give it all to God tomorrow!"

No wonder Jesus plopped a little child down in the middle of the circle when his disciples came up asking who was the greatest in the kingdom of heaven (Matt. 18:1–2). Children put us to shame in the area of joy that comes from pleasing God.

The next day, Enoch's dollar would pale in comparison to big-figure checks laid in the basket, but his joy would be as big as anyone's in the room. Our happiness never results from the number or size of the deeds we do in the kingdom, but from the enthusiasm with which we do them.

Attitudes Are Like Biscuits

Your mama probably told you what mine told me. When I was particularly agitated or particularly lazy or, heaven forbid, hungry, she told me I got up on the wrong side of the bed. That's what Mama said, but I say, "You ate the wrong biscuit." I mean, after all, you are what you eat.

Attitudes are like biscuits. Not all of them are good. I cooked for Daddy a good bit during the last few years of his life. It was a blessing to me that he had always liked food that was extremely well done, as in burned. I obliged with that menu preference. But he also liked bread with his meals. He once told me that wheat was his favorite vegetable. I'm better with cornbread than biscuits, but I tried. I remember he picked one up at supper one night, and said, "This would really be good," and I expected him to say, "with blackberry jelly." But back up. He said, "This would really be good to hit a rabbit with." (I think he grew up eating rabbit, and a biscuit would be a cheaper hunting tool than a gun.)

I wanted to tell him he wasn't so good in the biscuit department himself, as I happen to remember when I was a child, Mom had surgery and Dad was suddenly in charge of culinary arts. I heard an explosion one morning before school, and went into the kitchen where canned biscuits had joined the freedom movement of the day, had escaped the restrictions of the can, and were now stuck to the refrigerator, the phone book, the ceiling, and my sister.

Do not be slothful in zeal, be fervent in spirit, serve the Lord (Rom. 12:11).

Attitude Flavors

Not all biscuits make the cover of a Martha Stewart video, and not all attitudes are conducive to a joyful spirit. We can sing pretty loud, "I will work, I will pray, I will labor every day in the vineyard of the Lord," but do we say how we'll do it? With what attitude? There's a T-shirt I saw that said, "Sorry I'm late. I didn't want to come." I'm afraid that's jumped right off the shirt and landed in our pews, if not embedded itself in our hearts.

> I heard an explosion one morning.

Attitudes are not like Sonic shakes with endless combinations. Attitudes basically come in four flavors. Oh, people are complicated things, and there may be a multitude of reasons for the attitudes they carry. But at the heart they seem to all fit into one of four categories. So if you are what you eat, which biscuit did you have for breakfast?

I Can't

The following story is true. Some of the details have been changed to protect, well . . . everyone. In a church in the Carolinas, a group of Christians were standing around after an assembly laughing and talking and putting off going home since there's not much in life better than being with each other. As they began to wind down, a young man named Todd asked Trey, an elder, if he could see him in another room. In the meantime, Todd's wife Danielle and Trey's wife Felicia sat down to talk as well, and Danielle shared with Felicia the exact nature of the conversation in the other room.

I guess you're thinking since there was privacy involved, that this was a matter of grave concern. You would have guessed well, but guessed wrong. It really wasn't.

It was just a matter that the elders had asked the congregation to do for a short amount of time, just something so trivial that the details escape me. But here's the point. It was something along the lines of sitting in a certain place, or the order of assembly, or using a certain door, or staying an extended few minutes. It was that inconsequential, but still, somewhat inconvenient. No one, even the shepherds themselves, really wanted to do it, but it was just what they felt needed to be done for a time.

Danielle got right to the point with Felicia, but Todd shuffled his feet a while and beat around the bush, to the degree that Trey's heart was beginning to sink in dread of what might be coming. While they used different approaches, they both started with the same exact two words, "I can't."

Jesus wasn't too enamored with "I can't."

Let's get something straight. Can or can't has to do with possible or impossible. If someone asks me to pick up a mop and clean up a fresh mess, I could say "I can't," but it wouldn't be true. If someone told me to jump in the pilot's seat of an aircraft for an emergency medical flight, I could say with all sincerity, "I can't."

Moses got these two things mixed up in Exodus 3 and 4. He began to shuffle his feet and beat around the burning bush. He said things like "Who am I that I should do this?"; "What will I say?"; "No one will listen to me"; "I'm a little slow"; and finally, "Send someone else."

Ever seen a kid when he uttered something smart-alecky, and then horror overtook his expression? He realized he's said it now, and can't take it back! I wonder if that expression overcame Moses' face, for he had definitely said it now! And the next sentence says, "Then the anger of the Lord was kindled against Moses" (Exod. 4:14).

We really don't think it's a big deal if we say we can't be involved in some church work. We even group it with humility. We think someone else could do a better job. Wait, is there a straighter parallel line to the Moses account than that one?

Fast forward about fifteen hundred years or so, and Jesus wasn't too enamored with the "I can't" sentences either. He tells a parable in Matthew 25 in which those who gave an effort to increasing the talents they were given were rewarded, and heard the words,

> *Well done, good and faithful servant. You have been faithful over a little: I will set you over much. . . . Enter into the joy of your master (Matt. 25:21, 23).*

There is joy from working for the Master—now and later!

However, the one who did not put forth any effort, but buried his talents, was not greeted with, "Well, that's okay, I know you just didn't want to put yourself out there." No, this one was greeted with, "You wicked and slothful servant!" (Matt. 25:26). And, "Cast the worthless servant into the outer darkness. In that place, there will be weeping and gnashing of teeth" (v. 30).

I hate that I had to say that, but honestly, I didn't say it at all; Jesus Lord and Savior said it. He said it for our benefit, so that we would choose to try with all our being, knowing the results. We must never fail to act because we believe our acts will fail.

When we do that, it's really a trust matter. I am so incapable, but I'm going to step up to the plate anyway and put forth my best effort because God pinch hits whether or not there's a pinch, and "with God all things are possible" (Matt. 19:26).

Canned biscuits are not too good, but can't biscuits are worse. If Mama ain't happy, she might've eaten the "I can't" biscuit.

I Won't

That's the second attitude. It's the one the guy we call the rich young ruler had in Matthew 19. This is the unwilling attitude. It's not that we can't, but there is something asked of us that we don't want to do, so we won't.

Now most of us, even in the South, are tactful enough that when we are asked to do something in the work of the church, we generally do not raise our hands and say, "I won't do that." But there are a lot of ways to say, "I won't." The rich young ruler used one of them. He simply walked away (Matt. 19:22).

Don't do it. In trying to hold on to something, it cost him everything. We may say to ourselves that we could be involved in a work of the church, but right now we're trying to hold on to a career promise, a fitness goal, or maybe a sin we're just not ready to let go of. This commitment to church involvement would get in the way of those imminent priorities.

Wait, did we just get in a time machine and land at the feet of Jesus? Wake up! The story has ended for the rich young ruler. You and I have a chance to change ours! If there is something more important than doing the work of the Lord, the priorities are not just off-balance, they are completely whacked.

Walking away is a sorrowful thing (Matt. 19:22), and this is a book about happiness. We're aiming at doing the opposite of sorrowful things here. If there is an announcement to meet after worship if you're interested in helping with some need or work, you can run to it as Mark's account shows this young man doing in the "before" pictures, or you can just walk away and end up in the sad "after" pictures.

Another way we say "I won't" is simply to assume that someone else will. It's kind of how I say "we won" after an Alabama football game, and yet I didn't make a single touchdown or interception or squirt a water bottle into a player's mouth. I have the "we" mentality without being involved whatsoever.

We assume someone will teach the toddler class, someone will oversee the youth project, someone will pick up those who can't drive to worship, and some-one will even empty the trash can. You are a someone!

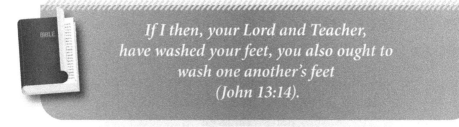

If I then, your Lord and Teacher,
have washed your feet, you also ought to
wash one another's feet
(John 13:14).

What about this? "It's not my job." How many times have we heard this? How many times have we said it? When Enoch was a baby, our family was visiting a congregation. Reiteration: This was not our home congregation. I dropped the kids off at their classes, and when I got to the cradle roll class, the teacher smiled, and said, "I am so glad to see you." I was feeling a little encouraged by the big welcome, and then she said, "Will you teach my class?"

To tell you the truth, my very first thought was, "That's not my job." I'm glad I had a second one. I buckled Enoch into his chair and moved to the center seat of the table and began singing songs about patting Bibles and wheels going 'round and 'round on the way to class.

Here's why. I enlisted as a soldier the day I became a Christian. What soldier is ever allowed to answer, "That's not my job," when given an assignment? If there is a job to be done and I am able to do it, and especially if I'm asked, it's my job.

"It's not my job."

But there is one way that we say "I won't" that far surpasses any other. It's by saying "I will" modified by the word, whether vocal or in thought, "later." Be careful; it's Satan's favorite tactic in getting us to join his team, because it's one that we will consistently fall for. We think we *will* ask someone to have a Bible study, we *will* host a youth devotional, we *will* teach a ladies' group or a children's class, but later. What is preventing us from doing it right now? Oh, I'm quite sure something is, whether it's a busy time of the year or we're just waiting until we know everyone a little better. The deal is, Satan is more than okay with you waiting until you get the proverbial round-to-it [ROUND TUIT].

It's like the couch my Aunt Eunice had. It was a hand-me-down when they got married, and after a few years, she wanted to replace it, but by then the children were small. If she got a new one, they would just spill Kool-Aid on it, and wear out the new springs. She would wait until they were older, but by the time the youngest one was sophisticated enough to appreciate a new one, the oldest one was married and had babies of his own. "Oh well," she said, "I'll wait until the grandchildren are older. I wouldn't want them to feel like they were in a museum and couldn't jump and play and spill." But as you guessed, great-grand-children came along before the youngest grandchildren were quite old enough to know how to treat a new couch. She would wait some more. The old couch was still sitting there when Aunt Eunice went to her heavenly reward.

And that's okay . . . when we're talking about couches, but tragic when we're talking about souls.

If Mama ain't happy, she might've put some fancy jelly on a plain old "I won't" biscuit.

I Will if I Have To

My least favorite attitude is, "I will if I have to." Please, I would rather you say "I won't."

One day, I found myself guilty of this, and as I was droning on about the things I had to do, my husband said, "Let me tell you something. One of these days, being a martyr is going to kill you." We both burst into laughter, but it was a reminder that no one enjoys being around a person who does things because he has to. If Mama ain't happy, she grabbed the "I will if I have to" biscuit.

What joy comes to anyone from doing something because you have to? Imagine if my husband brought me a bouquet of flowers, or even better, a bouquet of Heath bars on Valentine's Day, and when I became excited about it, he said, "I did it because I had to." Talk about a garbage can that would need emptying!

Don't imagine that God has any pleasure in my work for him if I am simply doing it because I have to. In the book of Malachi, God rebukes his people because their worship is wrong on so many levels, but mainly, it is wrong in attitude. At one point, he refers to them as they are bringing sacrifices as saying, "Oh, what a weariness!" (Mal. 1:13).

It sounds more familiar than it should. We can be quite busy in church work, but it is only the Lord's work when we do it with the right attitude. I have personally been guilty of saying, "Why am I always the one who ends up having to do this?" or "I hope I don't have to do this next time." There are those words: *have to*. Oh, what a weariness!

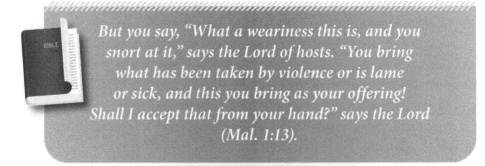

But you say, "What a weariness this is, and you snort at it," says the Lord of hosts. "You bring what has been taken by violence or is lame or sick, and this you bring as your offering! Shall I accept that from your hand?" says the Lord (Mal. 1:13).

The moment we hear ourselves and fix it, the moment we realize Jesus suffered on the cross and did not even have to, the moment we resolve to both enjoy these precious opportunities and allow others around us to see that we enjoy it, the burden is lifted. We're doing this because we want to, and we begin to see all the benefits we have because we "get to" work for the Lord. There simply is no other joy equal to that which comes from serving—when you want to.

I remember a camp counselor who every year exalted herself since she had to do this job because she was so needed. She would love to stay home, but she had to be at camp. My husband recruited the counselors, and just like anybody else in any arena, he wasn't interested in a worker who found no joy in it. So the next year, he didn't call her. We got by with the counselors we had, and no one missed her negative spirit. I mean, if Mama ain't happy, don't make her a camp counselor!

Oh, what a weariness!

Missing it that year changed her perspective and healed her attitude. She begged to come back the next year, and we never heard that she "had to" be there again. Let's evaluate our burden and realize it's a joy.

If Mama ain't happy, she got too big of a bite of the "I have to" biscuit.

I Want To

That brings us to our fourth and best attitude. It's the one the widow had in Luke 21:1–4 when she put in the treasury all that she owned. It's the one Mary had when she brought her very best to Jesus in John 12:3. It's the one David's three mighty men had when they heard David say he wanted a drink of water, and so on their own, they set out to make it happen, risking their lives by breaking into the camp of the Philistines and drawing water out of Bethlehem's well (2 Sam. 23:16). It's the one Robert and Mary have who still get excited, after forty-plus years in the Pacific islands, about every single soul who comes to Christ. It's the one my cousin Kyle had who, still recovering from a bout with an aggressive form of cancer and a regiment of difficult treatments, traveled to visit my daddy when he was weak in the hospital, and to encourage me as I sat bedside. I later learned Kyle had to park a block away, and in his words, didn't think he would make it, but he was all smiles when he got to the third floor. It's the one a California friend of mine had years ago when a woman was complaining about her toddler in a pawn shop, and this gentleman spoke up and said, "I'll take him." And to his surprise and joy, she accepted the offer, and he raised him.

It's the one Jesus had as he began to carry a heavy cross to his own crucifixion. It's the one he had as he carried a much greater weight of my sin, your sin, every sin since the garden. Unthinkable.

"Looking to Jesus, the founder and perfecter of our faith, who for the joy that was set before him endured the cross" (Heb. 12:2).

It would have meant nothing had he not done it willingly.

It turns out, there's only one biscuit fit to eat, and it's this one. Those who want to, despite the cost or the crisis, are the only happy people on the face of the earth. No one ever regretted doing the right thing.

If Mama ain't happy, she must've eaten the wrong biscuit.

 ## If You're Happy, You Will Know It

1. What are the first words of Malachi? How do the people respond to these words? How does our understanding or reaction to God's love determine the attitude with which we do his work?

2. How do we deal with people with the "have to" attitude? While there is a part of us that wishes they had not shown up, is that a flaw in our own attitude, and is there any effective way to nudge them into the right attitude? Share your thoughts.

3. Make a list of symptoms of the "martyr" attitude. Put a check beside those that would turn onlookers away from Christ.

4. Share a similar story to the one shared where the lady asked me to teach her class. What thing were you asked to do which, on one level, was conspicuously not your job? How did the story turn out?

5. Of the ways listed that we say "I won't" without forming the actual words, which one do you think is the most common? Which is the greatest temptation personally? What is another way we say "I won't"?

6. Is it true that if we are not asked to do a job that we are usually accustomed to doing, it deepens our appreciation for the involvement? The quarantine of 2020 was one event that resulted in many people appreciating church attendance more than ever before. What other lesser-known occurrence happened that caused you or others to miss a work you had taken for granted?

Happy Trails

And speaking of wheat . . .

I went to this group thing. I say that only because we were a group and it was a thing. We, as Christian ladies, get together once a month at 10:18. It's remarkable how everyone can show up at the exact same moment by announcing the time as eighteen minutes after the official time. We discuss things, as a group I mean, like spiritual training, health concerns, and the rising price of water chestnuts.

This particular morning, the topic was motivating your child in school. I wanted to be sure I arrived early at 10:17-and-a-half because this had become an issue of utmost importance in our lives. I don't want to overstate the case, but we have an eleven-year-old boy who someone recently, while visiting our home, mistook for a cactus.

This was only because he was working on pre-algebra, a fancy name for good old-fashioned confusion. The book was written by the same lawyers who write all that stuff before you hit the "I accept" box when you're installing spreadsheets and other shoot-em-up games on the PC. No one's expected to actually read that, right? I did once, and basically all I got out of it was that I wasn't supposed to tell anyone anything without prior notice to changing the rules within a reasonable amount of time subject to any charges void and nullified without upgrading at any time to charges that will apply only after the sole use expired until further notification. I'd say we all ought to be okay with that.

"Need any help with that?" I said, noticing that he had managed to write his name and what looked like part of a 3.

"Shhh! I'm concentrating!"

I was impressed. He had never concentrated before. I didn't notice the appendage in his ear.

Enter the dad. "Is Abram in a coma?"

"Shh! He's concentrating!"

"But he's never concentrated bef—-"

This was interrupted by a sudden burst of energy from the comatose cactus.

"INTERCEPTION!!!" He did the iguana dance all around his desk.

The Broncos lead by part of a 3.

You can see why the topic of motivation interested me, but the ensuing discussion disappointed me. I was expecting to find out that my son was suffering from a lack of motivation due to an inner turmoil or an external turmoil or some kind of turmoil. What I really found out was that it was ketchup.

All this time. Ketchup.

As you can imagine, this was an alarming discovery because we have controlling stock in all twelve ketchup companies. We have barges that float right up to our front door and unload, and still we find that supply cannot keep up with demand. Our dog requires that we season Ol' Roy with ketchup, and we have found that our children will even eat Brussels sprouts which have only half sprouted when served as a side to ketchup.

It had to be true because all of the other moms had found out that their children suffered in school for the same reason, and Nora had read a book about it "this thick."

Up until this point, I had thought ketchup was my friend. The doctor would look at my son. "He's growing. Is he eating his vegetables?"

"Oh yes," I would say. "Tomatoes."

But now I find out that one in 133 people have a gluten-related food allergy which affects their motivation.

"Wait a minute," I said. "If your son is a gluten victim and your son is a gluten victim and your son is a gluten victim, then the odds are in my favor! The next 397 people I meet will be gluten tolerant! Is this a great country or what? Bring on the Heinz!" I did the iguana dance. "This means my son is just lazy and distracted after all! What do you say we all go get some buffalo fingers?"

Thirty-four eyes peered at me over Jan Brady glasses.

"On a salad, I meant," calming down, "buffalo fingers on a salad. You know, cut up with artichokes and that stringy healthy stuff."

There was still silence.

"Glutenless, of course." My countenance was falling. I was down by part of a thirty-five.

"There are other factors, Celine."

I knew they were right. Now we could deal with self-esteem barriers, praise and reward, learning styles, and arranging conducive environments.

"There are many other gluten-based products."

I found out these were limited mostly to foods that taste good.

"All wheat is a danger, of course." Heads were nodding around the room to a beat that would have made the B-52's dizzy.

I made an inward resolve to provide healthier suppers for my family. Honeycomb night was definitely out the window.

The meeting ended, and we were still friends. Over lunch, we discussed more casual topics such as what we say to telephone solicitors and the two-day sale at the candle store, but I was a bit uneasy trying to hide my daughter's corndog by waving my napkin that direction while Nora popped a gladiola in her mouth.

Our viewpoints were different. It had happened before. It will happen again. Some of them walk to the beat of a different drummer while I can't hear a drum at all, but somewhere in the distance there's this squeeze box in a minor chord, and I struggle to do the iguana dance in rhythm. To paraphrase 1 Corinthians 12, they are hands and eyes, and I am a spleen.

Thank God for the hands and the eyes! These are the ladies who have cut out more construction paper loaves and fishes than the apostles passed out, and they still have twelve baskets remaining behind the filing cabinet in the teacher workroom.

But don't forget about the spleen either. Otherwise, whatcha gonna do with the gluten?

Originally published in Christian Woman *magazine, May/June 2007, revised 2021.*

11

IF MAMA AIN'T HAPPY,

She Thinks She Wants Some More

Greed or Contentment

Kim came over every day. It's what we did after kindergarten. I never considered that my mama was entrusted with an afternoon babysitting job; just that numbers and letters were over—time to head to the funhouse. Being the youngest of four, I had accumulated quite a stash of toys that had seen better days. You'd think we'd be content to each find a toy of choice and proceed to further the deterioration.

But I wanted to play with my sister's doll one day, and my sister was not there to protect the helpless victim. Kim wanted to play with it too. I mean she wanted to play with it bad, and the more I wanted to keep it, the more she wanted to take it from me. The more I knew she wanted it, the more valuable to me it became, and the tighter I held on to it. And so we kept it up. She pulled, and I held on tight.

I guess our fighting for it ended up in a new version of sharing. When the doll had taken all of the stress it could handle, Kim ended up with the head, and I ended up with the rest of it. (We obviously had not benefited from the story of King Solomon in Bible class.) My mama had begun to hear the shouting match followed by wails of despair at the plot twist, so she opened the screen door to find us standing on the carport holding vinyl body parts, and said, "Well, I hope you're happy!"

The deal is, we were not—sooo not!

Double the Fun: Get More

I should have learned something that day, standing there with what looked like the offspring of the headless horseman. It should have forevermore been apparent to me that happiness does not come from holding on tight to what we have, nor does it come from strongly wanting what others have.

Yeah, I should have learned it that day, but the truth is, it has taken years of battle scars, and I still struggle with the temptation to want more. I have New Testament passages encouraging me to rest in contentment, I have God's beautiful promises of wealth unimaginable in store for his faithful children, and I have shocking wake-up calls throughout scripture in the form of Bible examples of those who grabbed for the gusto and regretted it. What is wrong with me?

We are bombarded by the world's message: Get more things; be happier. But it's their word against his. Who are we gonna believe? Whose word do we trust?

If Mama ain't happy, she thinks she could be, if you'd just give her some more. Specifically, happiness is for sale at $19.99 a pop. And you can actually double the fun . . . if you order now. Pressure. Pressure to get twice as much. Now.

Among the things you could invest in? A plastic owl that makes supersonic sounds and whose red eyes flash. Mount him on your fencepost, and would-be tomato-eating deer and squirrels run for their lives, and who can blame them? I've seen more attractive diseased seaweed. Or how about a vacuum cleaner you stick in your ear? I mean, I've been told to do it a few times when there were no takers for tackling the den carpet, but for the same price, I think I'll go for the glue that bonds together things that are broken—as in most of my inventory. It literally shows a boat that was in two pieces suddenly healed at the seam and floating in the middle of the Chattahoochie or somewhere. I mean, who tried that thing out? "All right, let's get it out here in the depths of choppy waters far from civilization, where there just happens to be a camera crew, and see if it holds up."

The only thing that seems more ludicrous than actually entertaining the thought of becoming an owner of any of these things is the idea that you would somehow need two. Two owls! Two ear wax vacuum cleaners!

But the marketers are keenly aware of human nature. There's a promise of happiness in each pitch. I'd be happy if the deer quit eating my tomatoes. I'd be happier if I could hear you through all this earwax. And I'd certainly be happier if my boat were a one-piece instead of two.

Pray for Enough

We're in pursuit of more when we could be at peace with enough. Our prayers string together material wishes as if we've found a genie in a bottle. We ask for a better job, a newer car, a bigger house. James calls it asking wrongly.

> *You ask and do not receive, because you ask wrongly, to spend it on your passions (James 4:3).*

It's quite a contrast to the way Jesus taught us to pray. Matthew 6:11 says, "Give us this day our daily bread." In a give-me world, Jesus asks for bread—not the best bread or the most bread or a year's supply of bread—just today's portion. Luke 11:3 simply says to give it to us day by day.

We might repeat Jesus' words, but underneath them we whisper inside, "Let's make it a true daily double." Or triple. Or we'll take a lump sum now in multiples.

The Things of the World

I'm not saying, nor is scripture, that we can't have nice amenities or enjoy tangible gifts from others, but when I bite into the lie that there is happiness found in getting more, I've displaced my heart. First John 2:15 says, "Love not the world." We'll go along with that, especially in a time where the world holds turmoil and injustice, violence can break out without warning and evil gives birth to heartache time after time. We're not in love with this world, but don't miss the next phrase, "or the things in the world." That's the part that trips Mama up. After all, we just want to be happy, but the next part of the verse makes it clear there is absolutely no part of happiness along that route. "If anyone loves the world, the love of the Father is not in him."

Does it take a fire?

Christians get that we are happy because we have what the world does not have. We have the love of the Father in us. Why can't we get that we cannot attain happiness by getting what the world *does* have—things and more things? And while the getting is not condemned, the loving of the getting is. Let's look at the next verse. "For all that is in the world—the desires of the flesh and the desires of the eyes and pride of life—is not from the Father but is from the world" (1 John 2:16). Desire. Desire again. Pride. I missed the word happy; did you? But what I don't want to miss is this. When I spend my time and energy desiring, looking at what I want, and taking pride in possessions this side of eternity, I've landed my heart in the very thing I was trying to avoid—the world—and pulled away from the only source of lasting happiness—the Father.

What kind of wakeup call do we need? In our home, when we made the transition from a traditional digital type alarm clock that beeps you into consciousness to a virtual woman in a cylinder, our wakeup call shattered sleepful peace into frantic pieces. The first time that thing went off, I'm pretty sure my coronary system won an Olympic gold medal. I was jolted.

Will Your Treasures Burn?

We need that kind of wakeup call. The commercial and banter and—face it—Satan are tugging so hard to pull us from peace to pieces, we need to be jolted. And these two verses should suffice to do that.

It's really just that we've hit snooze on the matter anyway. Jesus already told us. Sometimes Jesus spoke in parables so that true seekers could experience the passion of the find, but not this time. Could it be any plainer than he put it in Matthew 6?

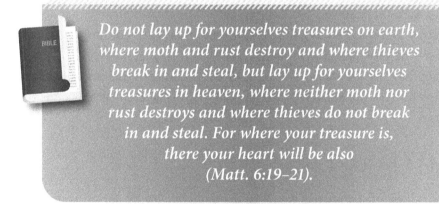

> Do not lay up for yourselves treasures on earth, where moth and rust destroy and where thieves break in and steal, but lay up for yourselves treasures in heaven, where neither moth nor rust destroys and where thieves do not break in and steal. For where your treasure is, there your heart will be also (Matt. 6:19–21).

You've been to a seminar somewhere that had an icebreaker phrased like this: "If your house caught on fire, and you had time to grab only one thing, what would it be?" I've asked this question a number of times across a spectrum of diverse groups. The answer is almost never something expensive. But rather, it's something that is full of meaning and symbolizes a nostalgia or an emotion we value. It's a box of photographs or something handmade by a grandmother or even just a note. Quite often it's a favorite copy of scripture. That's telling.

Does it take a fire? Does it really take our house in blazes to wake us up to the reality that monetary goods are meaningless? Let me tell you, there's going to be a fire, and it's not just going to take out your house, but your whole street, and the street next to it and . . . well, look at this:

> But the day of the Lord will come as a thief in the night, in which the heavens will pass away with a great noise, and the elements will melt with fervent heat; both the earth and the works that are in it will be burned up (2 Pet. 3:10 NKJV).

There's going to be a fire, and I can't grab one material thing from my house to take with me. I've never been so excited about a fire.

It means I get to move to a new place. Look through a real estate catalog and you'll quickly see that some houses are better than others. I don't really want the "starter home," the "fixer upper," or the one that says, "needs TLC." These don't really compare to the ones designed by master architects and built by the top tier of stone masons.

When the apostles were facing things hard for them to understand in John 14, Jesus said, "Let not your hearts be troubled." He then explained that he was going away, and that he was going to prepare a place for them—for us. Master architect. The very top tier of masons.

It appears that the happiest thought for the Christian is that her things here are going to burn up. What a joy to let go of the material in exchange for the immortal.

Greed's Consequences

But the saddest of all thoughts would be the thought of tying ourselves so much to the ash-destined that we forfeit the eternal euphoria.

There are so many lives recorded in scripture destroyed by the same kind of greed that meets us on every corner and in between YouTube videos. The rich young ruler went away sorrowfully, Judas hung himself, and I suspect Achan was really wishing for a do-over. But let's turn our attention to Gehazi. His story hits home because he was among the faithful. He had been a sidekick to Elisha, but sometimes, even among the faithful, the pull toward the material can be tragically powerful. And in 2 Kings 5, after Elisha had turned down a gift from the wealthy and grateful Naaman, the scriptures tell us this: "Gehazi, the servant of Elisha the man of God, said, 'As the Lord lives, I will run after him and get something from him'" (v. 20).

Running to get something from him. It hits home again. It sounds like the excitement of Black Friday and Cyber Monday rolled into one. But it turned into all the fun of Ash Wednesday.

Gehazi's material desire yielded to deception: lying and hiding the lies. In verse 25 he'd been "up the hill" to catch up to Naaman. Elisha asked him, "Where have you been, Gehazi?" And he said, "Your servant went nowhere." I've known some women who said almost the same words to their husbands, after agreeing not to spend any more money on clothes or shoes for a period of time. One specific memory comes to mind where the husband asked where his wife had been, and a shrug and "nowhere" popped out of her mouth as quick as it did for Gehazi. The truth is she'd been "up the hill" to the factory outlets.

> I get to move to a new place.

For Gehazi, the consequences show up two verses later when he is told, "The leprosy of Naaman shall cling to you and to your descendants forever" (2 Kings 5:27).

Greed can have "forever" consequences, and a displaced focus on material things over spiritual will surely influence little ones in our homes until it becomes a leprosy handed down from generation to generation. It's the Gehazi factor. No one's ever gotten happiness from it, most especially Mama.

If Mama ain't happy, she might be pulling the doll head so hard it's about to pop off. She could let go of it and find out what Paul told Timothy a couple of thousand years back:

Godliness with contentment is great gain
(1 Tim. 6:6).

 ## If You're Happy, You Will Know It

1. How relevant are the ancient words of Matthew 6:19–21? What specific instances have you experienced where these exact things happened to your things, or the things of those close to you?

2. The incident with Gehazi is chosen to illustrate greed, though a few other contenders are mentioned. Select one of these other than Gehazi, or another Bible character not even mentioned, and see how the temptations that led to their downfall parallel our own. Find something specific in their story that has not changed over the thousands of years that separate us.

3. Gehazi's faithfulness is also mentioned in this chapter. Find every time that this servant is mentioned, and what he did. How many of these things are exemplary things?

4. Look up the verse that follows 2 Peter 3:10. If point A is that all our "valuables" are going to burn up anyway, how does that lead to point B, and what is point B?

Happy Trails

And speaking of the youngest of four . . .

Our first was due December 23. Somehow all the relatives had in mind that at two days old, he would run down the stairs with squeals of delight at the toys Santa had left on Christmas morning. Turns out, it was his first of a host of standoffs. He refused to arrive by Christmas, or New Year's Eve, or New Year's Day, or the Alabama bowl game. How about, say, a night with a record-setting temperature-drop at 4:04 AM? Yeah, that's about right.

And so by early November we had tons of Baby's First Christmas bibs, sleepers, ornaments, wrapping paper, and diaper rash cream, all obsolete by the baby's arrival January fourth. So we were thinking we would box these things up along with the ceramic tree and glitter-glued stockings, get them out next year, and the baby would be set. It's why we have a fifth of the tree every Christmas dedicated to a year, engraved on ornaments, in which nothing at all happened.

We also failed to factor in that these same relatives who were excited about baby's first Christmas the first time were doubly excited about baby's first Christmas the second time because now it was real. There was an actual baby with it, crawling around like a demolition crew complete with radar. He could detect when the toilet lid had been left up and when the paperwork had been properly filed again.

So now the "baby's first" items came on with a new fervor. It was like everyone we had ever met or waved at must have bought out the infant department at the after Christmas Sale in January while I was in labor.

We had to change his outfit seven times a day to get all of them worn by Christmas. They all had the same phrase, and even though he was gifted, he couldn't read a single one of them.

And when the big day arrived, everyone was ready with a slew of wagons, swing sets, and remote-control dancing rabbits. He woke up with a fever and swollen eyes. He tried to comply with the festivities, but it was all he could do to lick a candy cane.

Now there's a onesie for you! If you want to sell a baby item that's sure to be accurate, why not have it say something like "Baby's first stomach virus," "Baby's first diamond ring flushed," "Baby's first spit up on a congressman."

By the next Christmas, there was another baby, and she probably got three ornaments, as opposed to twenty-nine. The babies came as the Christmases rolled by until the fourth baby's first Christmas came along. He got—I promise—a toilet brush. We could think of nothing that suited him better since his favorite activity was playing with the one we already had.

We were just as thankful, just as overwhelmed by the joy of the little one on this occasion. It's just that by the time the fourth one makes a crash landing, the logistics of everything change. I know; I was fourth of four.

My constant complaint was, "They get to do everything, and I don't get to do anything." Their constant complaint to this day, is still, "You got away with everything."

Everything I ever owned was handed down. I wanted a new lunchbox worse than anything except a horse. I wanted a Holly Hobbie lunch box, not the rusted one with airplanes on it. But I received a pat on the head, and the consolation, "But you have older brothers and sisters. You wouldn't trade them for a lunch box, would you?"

Hmmm, new lunch box or the people who say, "Sorry, only three swings on this swing set, but you can rake leaves if you want; that's a lot more fun." A lunch box or someone to eat the bacon before you get to the table? A lunch box or three votes against *Captain Kangaroo*, and for *Bonanza* reruns instead? I should have had a bumper sticker, "If one prevail against him, two shall withstand him" (Eccl. 4:12 KJV). It was my life in a nutshell.

Now that I'm on the parenting end, I have a new perspective. You spend three weeks making a costume for the first child, try it on him three or four times, keep adding accents, and burn four rolls of film on it. By the fourth, you say, "Costume? Is that today?" and quickly grab a garbage bag, cut the neck out, throw it over him, run a piece of masking tape down the middle and clap, "Yea! You're a road!"

You iron the first child's baseball uniform and add color boost so he'll be ready for the camera when he gets up to bat. By the fourth, you convince him to slide in the dirt when he first gets out of the car. "That way," you explain, "the dirt will be fresh and everyone will think you've already played a game. I promise no one will know we didn't have time to wash the uniform."

The first child brings a backdrop with glued-on hand-cut letters and photos explaining the life cycle of his turtle for share day at Cub Scouts.

By the fourth, you are scrounging for items in the glove compartment on the way, and you say, "Socks! Socks are interesting."

The first child's Bible class teacher gets homemade fudge for Christmas, wrapped up in cellophane with curly ribbon and a handmade card. We won't even bring up the time the fourth child's Bible class teacher got shoe polish. Hey, it was unopened and the store was closed the night before. Everyone needs shoe polish, right? Back me up on this.

Fourth children fear that if they don't come in with a wrecking ball, no one will notice them at all, and so our fourth wore the nickname "Master Blaster of Disaster" the first five years of his life. If it couldn't be broken, it's only because he hadn't seen it yet.

Notice that proverb in Ecclesiastes continues a few verses down to say, "A threefold cord is not quickly broken."

But throw a fourth one in there, and it's history.

Originally published in Christian Woman *magazine, November/December 2014.*

12

IF MAMA AIN'T HAPPY,

Her Funny Bone's Broken

Losing It or Laughing about It

I was in a china shop in London. I couldn't make up a more high-brow place for this to happen if I had tried. It was arranged not so much in aisles, but as if it were a formal parlor. All was silent, except for a subdued backdrop of classical music. The store was devoid of patrons except for a few future brides trying to select the most elegant pieces for their registry. A friend accompanied me, and I don't really know what happened while we were admiring dainty teacups. I don't remember at all, but whatever it was seemed hysterical at the time. And so, as you've guessed, we burst helplessly into sustained laughter—the kind where you can't seem to inhale, but once you do, you do it so that all for blocks around are aware of it. We were somewhere just between doubling over and wetting our pants when the well-groomed merchant approached us and asked if she could help us find something. We tried so hard to answer. We really did, but all we could do was shake our heads and wave with our hands to let her know we were finding everything just fine.

Let me take this opportunity to apologize to all Americans for representing our country that day. What happened next was priceless. She said in a British accent that carried the essence of the queen herself, "Well, I'm glad you girls are having such a fine time in our store." If the laughter volcano had not fully erupted before, let me assure you that this put us at a nine out of eight on the explosivity scale.

The thing is, I think she genuinely meant it. There was no condescending or irritated tone in her voice. It seemed that if she couldn't be part of the good time, she at least was glad to provide the venue.

Strength and Sanity from Joy

In the book of Ecclesiastes, we read that there is a time to weep, and a time to laugh (Eccles. 3:4). Mama has to do both if she's going to maintain her sanity. In this chapter, we'll examine those times to laugh. I contend that for the forgiven Christian, they are often. I reflect frequently on the laughter—*mirth* in the KJV—that God wanted his people to experience in Nehemiah 8 after their repentance. It's from this passage that we learn that the joy of the Lord is our strength (Neh. 8:10). Not worldly joy, not self-seeking pleasure, but the joy of the Lord. It often comes out in our laughter. And where does Mama need that laughter the most?

Laugh for the Sake of the Old

Sometimes life gives us the privilege of caring for an older person we love. It's a hefty weight on our shoulders, not because of the time or effort involved, but because of the knowledge of the responsibility. The questions plague our souls: Are we doing it right? (Most of us have never done it before.) Did we remember all the medications? Are enough safety measures in place? And wait, is this garbage day?

It can consume our thoughts to the point of exhaustion. We don't need that because the exhaustion part comes on full-force without invitation via lifting, hopping up through the night, burning the road from our house to theirs, and an endless list of near ridiculous things we could not make up.

Do you know what I believe these older people in our care need as much as they need the medication or the nutrient supplements or the orthopedic inserts? They need joy and laughter. Laugh for the sake of the old.

Welcome Laughter in Adversity

The challenges are real and taxing. Some of our parents are imprisoned by mental disorders that impede their ability to see the humor. Laugh anyway. It will help you relax which will make you a better caregiver.

I would never suggest that we would sink to laughing at the affliction of another. But neither would I say that laughter is not welcome in the midst of such adversity. Some days we just need to sit down and laugh with our loved one. And one day Dad and I dressed up like cows to get free food at Chick-fil-A. Not everyone can say they've pushed a cow in a wheelchair. But I can. Life gave me another opportunity to laugh or cry during the outing, as it started sprinkling on both heifers. (We had nursing gloves attached to us for udders.) I got him transferred from the chair to the car as quickly as I could, but it still took the better part of a presidential vote recount to accomplish it. But that was nothing compared to the time it took me to lift the chair into the trunk of the car. After several attempts and a near-broken Holstein back, even I, world's tightest cheapskate, was second-guessing if free chicken nuggets were worth it. In telling this to my husband over the phone, we had a laugh track on both ends of the conversation, and I said, "I was sweating like a pig!" He answered, "Yeah, but you were dressed like a cow, working like a dog, getting mad as a hornet, and hungry as a horse." It's a day I'll forever put in the happy column.

> I was making cheese toast and calling it breakfast.

One of the memories I wouldn't trade for a lifetime supply of dark chocolate is the hearing aid episode. Dad's was on the blink, and he couldn't hear thunder. I was trying to call the audiologist, but couldn't think of her name. I was also making some cheese toast, and calling it breakfast because Dad wanted to be there, wherever it was, before it opened. He was making up his bed; something he did till the day he died. He had to hold on to each piece of furniture in the room as he circled the bed to tuck the sheets and fluff the pillow, but he got it done as I stood ready to spot him.

The Joy of Burnt Cheese

"Dad, I don't think I can get you in there until I call them, and I can't call them until we know who to call. Do we have any paperwork with a name?" We came up with a few guesses, but none of them sounded right, and then I said, "Cheese toast!" I ran to the oven to retrieve the toast. The cheese slices had ballooned up into a parachute, and they were just before the crackling stage. Dad liked near-burnt food, which came in handy for me more than once.

Did you save it in time?

I sprinted back to the bedroom because I didn't like to get far out of range during the bed-making routine. I said, "I'm sorry, Dad, I almost forgot the cheese toast, but we've got to think of the audiologist's name." He snapped to attention, and said, "Is it Black?"

"You know, it may be," I said as I scrolled and scrolled through the phone book. "I can't find a Dr. Black here."

Dad responded, "What about the toast? Is it black or did you save it in time?"

I laugh about it still. Those were golden days no one can rob me of, but if I had not laughed, they might have been a little more cankered rust than gold. We could never seem to get off the obstacle course. It could take ten minutes or more to get up a short set of steps. And by the time we finished a bath and moved into physical therapy, I felt like I needed both worse than he did. And while I never had to experience Dad not knowing who we were or where he was—my soul stirs for those who do—just the short-term occasional memory lapses ignited my worry beast.

Broken Funny Bone

All of these compounded by lack of sleep and neglected schedules are enough to snap the fragile strength of any caregiver, and there are some who are stuck in that brittle position because they haven't found the laughter. Look for it. It's hiding behind the stern heroism. There are the martyrs so entrapped by their grave responsibility that every challenge is a defeat. If Mama ain't happy, she might be one of them. If Mama ain't happy, she needs to put her funny bone in a cast; it's broken.

Yes, it's for our own sanity we need to laugh. But even more so, it's for our aged ones. They often feel burdensome. Ease it. Have fun. When all else is slipping away from you and you can't help it, God hands you a gift you can share with your loved one that helps the two of you cope with it all together. Laugh for the sake of the old.

All the days of the afflicted are evil, but the cheerful of heart has a continual feast (Prov. 15:15).

Laugh for the Sake of the Young

It's no secret; parenting is not for wimps. We had three kids in three years, five months. What were we thinking? Obviously not enough about what's on the family planning aisle of the supermarket. We had the fourth one three years later. Of course we knew we were richer than Oprah at a cash windfall. Yes, we do believe Psalm 127:3–5 concerning children, heritage, quiver, and all that stuff! Or as I said when I was little, "Happy is the man whose gizzard is full of them."

But when you have four people running around from the height of "get a black eye running into the high chair" all the way down to "eating Cheerios out of the air vents," it gets a little hairy. You feel like if you see one more allergy treatment commercial where pristine children dressed in unstained clothing are skipping in slow motion through flower gardens, holding the hands of smiling adults, and licking ice cream cones, you'll call the number on the screen, all right. You'll call and say, "Hello, I'm on Planet Earth with real children with overactive voice boxes. What planet did you film this on? How do you get children to do anything in slow motion? And why hasn't the ice cream dripped down every piece of clothing until it oozed through the eyelets of the shoe to soak the socks. I'll take a box of that allergy-med stuff if it works these wonders. Cost is no object."

Heart Medicine

The deal is, that kind of medicine doesn't work. Oh, it might work for allergies. I don't know anything about that, but it doesn't slow children down or calm the tempest called parenting. But there's a different medicine I'll invest the whole purse in. Proverbs 17:22 says, "A joyful heart is good medicine." How does the joyful heart operate?

How does the joyful heart operate?

It remembers what is valuable. It praises God. It prays hard. It speaks kindly. But falling just under these tenets, it laughs. I was on the seasonal aisle of the store today, and Valentine's Day is just around the corner. There stood a mama of many. One child was in the ordinary, where-a-child-is-supposed-to-sit part of the shopping cart, one was in the where-the-groceries-go part, a third was down in the where-the-huge-bag-of-dogfood-goes part, and the oldest was standing beside her trying to push the cart. Everybody had learned how to talk by now, but not one of them had learned how to stop talking. Each was pretty opinionated about which box of valentines they should buy. The oldest simply repeated, "When are we ever going to leave?" And the mom just laughed. She thought it was a great question, bellowed again when she repeated it, and said, "Whenever they choose some valentines."

I wanted to applaud and give her an award. No one will go away with a bad memory of a horrible day in a discount store. Four adults will one day look back, whether they remember this episode or not, on childhood days filled with a mother's laughter. Laughter on a store aisle, when put in that perspective, might be a nudge toward an eternal destination. Laugh for the sake of the young.

I have seen other mothers in the same harried circumstances scream at the children, be rude to innocent bystanders, or just about break down in tears. If you're a mother, you get it. You really do. But no mother ever said, "I wish I had laughed less and stressed out more." Laugh for the sake of the young.

There are children who have suffered from Shaken Baby Syndrome. It is a literal crying shame. When Solomon penned "a time to laugh and a time to cry," he might have had this occasion in mind for crying, loud and long. But the moments before the baby was shaken, those were the moments when the medicine should have been in reach—the joyful heart. That was the time for laughing. I remember reading about Erma Bombeck, renowned humorist in her time and mother of three, visiting a women's wing of a prison where she was told by a mother, "If I had known I could laugh, I might not be here today."

He will yet fill your mouth with laughter
and your lips with shouting
(Job 8:21).

Why Treasure Laughter?

The challenges of parenting are monumental. A field officer does not carry the weight of a mother. Someone is trained at any time to take his place. No one can take my place or yours in parenting, and truth be told, there is no training that prepares us for duty. The field is named Chaos, the terrain is rocky, and the tank is just short of impossible to maneuver. But God entrusted us with the position, and then it's as if he said, "Here's something you're going to need in your back-pack that will lighten it," and gave us laughter. I mean, an endless supply. Money runs out at the end of the month. Laughter doesn't. The years fly by and are gone.

Laughter sits down and keeps you company. Crises may come rampantly, but they leave just as surely as they came. Laughter outstays them every time.

I got three dents in our brand new mini-van the day we brought it home from the dealer—two from baseballs, and one from a bat. All were accidents, so why not laugh?

During a Christmas dinner party with seventy-two people from the community, my kids went racing for a ball that rolled under the bed. A guest child got caught on a glue trap we had hidden under there because we suspected a mouse. Our suspicions were correct because when we pulled the kid out, we pulled a mouse out with him. It could have been a terribly stressful moment had it not been so hilarious.

You can't laugh away disobedience. or disrespect.

My small children were thrilled to have an "Italy" party in which they learned all about the country, and each was allowed to invite an elderly couple from church. They chose to make and serve spaghetti, and the first plate out of the kitchen was served promptly and swiftly right into the lap of one of the guests of honor. We all could have cried, especially the elderly gentleman, but it's so much more fun to laugh. Pretty sure no one was going to forget it ever, but this way, the memory was attached to joy and not regret, embarrassment, or shame for the child.

I have a part-time photography business, and we try to laugh our way through children's sessions. Children are often ill or hungry, tired or frustrated, and so what sometimes happens is that the parents threaten them that if they don't smile, they won't get to have their special treat—or whatever—you fill in the blank. It's a bad day, but it didn't have to be. If Mama's not happy, she fails to see the humor. And that is failure indeed.

When the Mourning Comes

Laugh for the sake of the young, even when you can't laugh with the young. There are times when children push the limits, and we have to be firm. You simply can't laugh away disobedience, disrespect, or as they get older, the temptation to willfully sin.

Scripture even reminds us, "Let your laughter be turned to mourning" (James 4:9). It becomes clear when the passage is addressed in its entirety that it's written to someone tampering with sin, trying to be friends with the world and still be blessed by God. James calls it adultery (v. 4), and it's simply not funny. It goes in the "time to cry" column.

Fast, parents. Pray. Cry. Trust. And while you allow God to shoulder the burden you can't seem to budge, allow yourself some laughter behind closed doors. You have to laugh some. You just must. I remember a recent struggle some of our closest friends, George and Julia, were going through with their children. We would cry together, pray together, and most certainly laugh to get through. We knew things would get better—that's trust! But before they got better, they got worse—that's trial. I remember the load being so heavy at one time that I feared Julia would lose her gift of seeing the humor—I feared the times were so dark that there was no humor left to see. I prayed that God would sustain her ability to laugh. That's when she picked up the phone and called me, and as we got deep into the phone call, we belly-laughed, and I was reassured that the joy of the Lord is our strength that Satan can't touch.

Laugh for the Sake of the Gospel

The gospel is good news. Good news doesn't hang out with killjoys. The terms are contradictory. As we see the good news unfold to hearer after hearer in the book of Acts, we begin to see a recurring theme of gladness, rejoicing, and much joy.

> And day by day, attending the temple together and breaking bread in their homes, they received their food with glad and generous hearts (Acts 2:46).

> Then they left the presence of the council, rejoicing that they were counted worthy to suffer dishonor for the name (Acts 5:41).

> So there was much joy in that city (Acts 8:8).

> The eunuch saw him no more, and went on his way rejoicing (Acts 8:39).

The incredible thing is that the backdrop was often an unpleasant one: prison, persecution, beating—at the very base a heart-rending conviction of killing the Son of God. If Mama ain't happy, is she wrestling with something God can take care of? In every case in Acts, when conviction led to cleansing, it immediately turned the situation from desperate to celebratory. It echoes the passage we alluded to earlier in Nehemiah. "And all the people went their way to eat and drink and to send portions and to make great rejoicing, because they had understood the words that were declared to them" (Neh. 8:12).

Have we understood the words that were declared to us? "And Peter said to them, 'Repent and be baptized every one of you in the name of Jesus Christ for the forgiveness of your sins, and you will receive the gift of the Holy Spirit'" (Acts 2:38). If we understand this, no matter the circumstances—beating, imprisonment, or a flat tire on a lonesome highway in the noonday sun—we will make great rejoicing. Laugh for the sake of the gospel.

Laugh because the Mood Is the Only Thing You Can Change

When you're staring through the window at your car keys lying on the seat of a locked vehicle, you can stomp and rant; lots of strangers can come and give you advice; you can scratch the edge of your door and tear up all that rubber stuff around it; but none of that will do you a bit of good. Grieving the situation does not change one thing about it. Sometimes the only thing you can do that will truly help is laugh. It won't cause the keys to levitate and come out the exhaust pipe, but it will make a bad day so much better. You won't need a knife to cut the tension anymore; it will dissipate. Relationships of those there with you will be strengthened instead of strained. And it is all within your power. You decide. If Mama ain't happy, she chose poorly.

It reminds me of the time my sister locked her keys in her car and called me to rescue her. After weighing several options, we chose to go to her house thirty miles away to retrieve the spare. It didn't occur to us that the house would be locked, and the key to it was on the same key ring locked in her car. But something else occurred to me, and it occurred to me at the exact moment that I was holding the extension ladder for her to climb over a second-story railing. It occurred to me that this was the deep-down kind of hilariousness, the kind that makes your whole body shake when you are trying to steady a ladder.

Last night, I was bragging about my new purse. I think something like four times between the church building and the restaurant, I said something about how much I liked that thing, what a great deal it was, and how many neat compartments it has. I hopped up to go to the bathroom soon after we ordered. I guess the fact that I had mentioned all those compartments made my husband a little curious himself. So he pulled on one of the front zippers, and apparently, it was made not just to pull, but to pull off. When I came back, he was frantically working with that purse zipper, but to no avail. I asked, "What are you doing?" and he said, "Breaking your new purse." Disappointed? Slightly. Tempted to gripe about either the purse or the husband? You bet. But the truth is, it was funny. Griping would change nothing about the broken zipper. I couldn't change that. The only thing within my control was to have a good time or a bad time. If Mama ain't happy, she fails to see the humor in a busted new zipper and a husband desperately trying to make it unhappen.

Laugh because God Is Good to You

We ought to be ashamed to walk around in a climate-controlled environment with a roof overhead and most of all, our sins washed away, and wear frowns on our faces. In Psalm 126, God had brought his people back from Babylonian captivity, and the response was,

> *Then our mouth was filled with laughter,*
> *and our tongue with shouts of joy;*
> *then they said among the nations,*
> *"The Lord has done great things for them"*
> *(Ps. 126:2).*

I couldn't bring it home to us any more than the next verse does: "The Lord has done great things for us; we are glad" (v. 3). No matter what kind of day we are having, and they can range from little things like a stomach virus or chocolate-covered cashmere all the way to the unthinkables: cancer, divorce, ICU, heartbreak. But the bottom line is, the Lord has done great things for us. He has brought us out of sin's captivity, and in the words of verse 1 if you back up, it's like a dream.

Yes, as Ecclesiastes 3:4 tells us, there is a time to weep. Jesus did it (John 11:35; Luke 19:41). Ruth and Naomi did it (Ruth 1:9). All of God's children have done it from the dawn of time, and John 11:35 shows us that sometimes when we cry, God cries.

> The Lord has done great things for us.

But by the very wording of the Ecclesiastes verse, we know that since there is a time to cry, there is a time not to. In fact, many of the times that man is found crying in scripture, God directs him to reevaluate his situation, to get up, get right, or get busy (Josh. 7:10; Hosea 12:4–6; John 20:15–17).

When we get up, get right, and get busy, I argue that Christians have a deep-down laughter that the world can't comprehend. We laugh on the outside because our soul is laughing. We don't return to a void once the chuckles have died down. Oh, there is a range of emotions that God gave us, and so he deeply understands and connects to our sadness. But he sent the Savior to provide for us an overriding and constant joy that takes us through the valleys. Peter is discussing those valleys when he says, "rejoice with joy inexpressible and full of glory" (1 Pet. 1:8).

Our Genesis sister, Sarah, who knew some of those same trials we do, said, "God has made laughter for me; everyone who hears will laugh over me." Is it not true for his daughters thousands of years removed? He has given us laughter, and it is contagious to those around us.

The world is watching our response to our trials. If Mama ain't happy, I hope she'll make up her mind to laugh. I hope all around us will notice, if only to say, "I'm glad you girls are having such a fine time in our store."

> *Do not be grieved, for the joy of the Lord is your strength (Neh. 8:10).*

If You're Happy, You Will Know It

1. Read aloud the following examples of joy in the book of Acts: 11:23; 13:48; 13:52; 15:3; 15:31; 16:34; 21:7. What was the backdrop of each?

2. Set a one-minute timer, and write down all the emotions you can think of in that time. Go back and circle the ones you have experienced the most in recent days. How does the transcending joy of Christ affect or help you deal with those emotions?

3. Read Psalm 126 in its entirety. What is the relationship between sadness, joy, and laughter? Which phrase in this psalm speaks to you the most. What event in your life parallels the captivity, and in what moment in your life did you experience the laughter kind of joy pictured here?

4. Look back on your day so far today. Make a list of the things that did not go as planned. In another column, list all the ways God has blessed you. Which list is longer? Which list will you focus on?

5. Surely every person reading this has locked the keys either in her car or her house. Recount that story to yourself, or if this is a group study, let everyone share. What was the funniest part of the episode?

6. There are five "Laugh because" or "Laugh for the sake of" segments in this chapter. Which of these do you think is the most important, and why?

7. How far do the ripples of laughter go? My own laughter helps me personally at the moment, and we probably agree that it helps those nearby at the time, but does it go beyond the immediate occasion? Does it go even beyond those parameters? If so, how, and who all could possibly be affected?

8. Are there times so dark in parenting that laughter is off the table? Have you specifically experienced times when the laughter escaped you, or have you experienced times when the laughter was the only thing (aside from prayer) that got you through?

9. Do you know someone going through difficult parenting, caregiving, or other life-challenging times? Provide them with some laughter; they need it! Go grab some coffee together this week and laugh all you can. (Get a mutual friend or someone from your youth group to keep kids for just an hour.) Bring a favorite relatable meme or two, and after all the laughter, pray together before returning to the battlefront.

10. Read James 4. In what ways were the readers of James's letter out of control? How does seeing this help us better understand his directive to "let your laughter be turned to mourning"?

11. Do a little online research this week. What are the health benefits of laughter?

12. Read 1 Corinthians 13:4–7. Which of these love characteristics commonly pair up with laughter?

13. Are you a parent of multiple young kids? There is a lot of humor in your world that we often miss. At the end of the day today, spend ten minutes texting yourself all the funny things the kids did or said. Then pray that you will value the humor each day.

14. Do a personal study of joy in Acts. What is the backdrop each time we find the word?

15. Which happens more: laughing in a time and place that we shouldn't, or not laughing in a time and place that we should?

Happy Trails

And speaking of Americans . . .

The first thing we need to straighten out in order to get a handle on American history is the difference in the British Revolution and the British Invasion. In the British Revolution, Paul Revere the Great rode around on a horse, screaming about the British and ruining their surprise party. His English was very good because he was from England. In the British Invasion, Paul Revere the Eccentric rode in playing an electric organ and screaming about Arabian Nights. His English was not as good, as he mostly said things like, "Louie, Louie, oh baby, me gotta go."

The next thing we need to establish is the difference between the kind of tea parties they had in Boston and the kind they have in the playroom upstairs. The first problem with the Boston kind is that they invited the boys, and that turned out to be disastrous. Whereas girls do sensible things like put beads on the teddy bears and sip invisible liquid with their pinkies held out, the boys come in and create complete havoc throwing enormous boxes of tea directly into the ocean.

I learned most of these facts on a field trip my son took with his school to a Revolutionary War reenactment in south Alabama. We found out immediately why the Revolutionary soldiers dressed in tight white knee-pants. This was in case they got called on by the tour guide to carry the flag for their colony. This works out much better than wearing your brother's hand-me-down jeans, which are what my son wore, because the jeans tend to be two inches too big in the waist and slip down while both your hands are hoisting a flag and there is not an extra one to hoist the pants.

It was about 1776 degrees that day, and we took a miserable hike to every part of the thirteen colonies, and I'm pretty sure, embarked on a fourteenth. We finally stopped on Betsy Ross's porch where she was selling lemonade to offset the rising price of needles and thread. I asked how much for something wet for my parched throat. It was one dollar if by land, and two if by sea, but they wouldn't accept my John Hancock on the check to pay for it.

I struggled along following the boy with his pants around his ankles. We stopped in the beauty shop where George Washington and Samuel Adams were getting new ponytails. We also enlisted in boot camp where we learned how to carry a rifle properly, but I was pretty sure if we ever had to use the thing, we were toast since it was little more than a stick without even a working trigger. We posed for pictures in stocks to remind us of the consequences should anyone consider sneaking a cup of lemonade without proper payment. We viewed ballroom dancing in a parlor which, when the boys got involved, looked more like London Bridge Is Falling Down than like My Fair Lady. Again, there were dainty biscuits and punch available, but none for the chaperones who forgot to bring cash. The policy was pretty clear—it was no hydration without cash representation.

It was clear we had all brushed up on our American history on the way home as I went immediately and directly to a drive-through without passing Congress, pulled a few Articles of Confederation out of my purse before wildly waving my debit card, and ordering, "Give me lemonade or give me death."

13

IF MAMA AIN'T HAPPY,

Check the Bag of Flour!

Mixing in Self-Rising
Or All-Purpose

We have this box in the refrigerator. I bet you do too. It's a goldy-orange color, and has, of all things, an arm on it. And a hammer. I don't even get that. I mean, shouldn't that be on the side of a tool chest or the license plate of a construction truck or something? What is it about sprinkling a little baking soda over some flour in a mixing bowl that would conjure images of muscling and demolition?

And does anybody bake with baking soda? I don't think I ever have. But we continue to buy a box, tear open the lid somewhere around the perforations but never ever actually on them, set it in the fridge, and feel that we are healthy and responsible consumers. The box stays there through a couple of presidential elections or until someone gets a bee sting or has to explode something for fourth-grade physical science, hence its nickname in our home—volcano in a box.

I have friends who buy it, and—get this—pour it directly down the drain. If you've got that kind of money—sixty-seven cents—can I also interest you in some very expensive cookie dough to fund the softball trip?

Self-Rising Resembles Self-Righteous

I guess one of the reasons that I have no idea of the purpose of baking soda— other than to sit in the fridge until the moisture glues the cardboard to the plastic shelf—is that we use self-rising flour around here. We do not sift; we do not combine dry ingredients; we do not make a well for the wet ingredients—we just dump!

And it somehow makes food just the same. We don't need the other stuff. It's self-rising.

I thought when I got married I would need baking powder—a first cousin to baking soda, but it lives in the pantry instead of the fridge. It was a cute little can with a picture of a woman from colonial times, and I think that's probably the last time anyone actually used it. It's affectionately named Clabber Girl, and which one of us wouldn't be flattered by the endearing term? I'm on my second can of Clabber Girl now in a long-running marriage. This is not because I used up the first can, but because I would be embarrassed if anyone asked how long I had owned the first can. The only thing that's been in the kitchen longer is the turmeric. (Don't ask; I have no idea.)

When it comes to baking, we use the self-rising flour. It's easier that way. Truth be told, it's probably not as good as what our grandmothers turned out with the all-purpose flour. They spent more time on it, knew how much a pinch was, and took great care in getting it right.

I don't, which is usually why . . . it isn't. And if Mama ain't happy, she might not have the right bag of flour. Not in the kitchen, but in her heart, which gets in the mixer with her life. What is it about a self-rising attitude that makes it the wrong bag of flour? Self-rising flour doesn't need anything else. It is self-sufficient. And I guess if it's going to heap up in the bowl and come over the sides, it's going to have to do it on its own.

Do you know someone who exalts herself? Isn't she miserable? I guess sometimes we see it as the easy way to get the result we want, but it's a much more inferior result than even the bag of self-rising flour yields. Jesus himself told us,

> *Whoever exalts himself will be humbled,*
> *and whoever humbles himself will be exalted*
> *(Matt. 23:12).*

The All-Purpose Way

In contrast, there's the all-purpose bag of flour, and the all-purpose way of life. When Mama uses this bag, she mixes right in there with others, working for the best results possible. She is all-purpose. Whenever a need arises, she tries. She prays, she comforts, she mops, she drives, she googles, she gives, she texts, she picks up, she drops off, and then she prays some more. It's a loose paraphrase of Proverbs 31. We can't do it all, but we can do all we can.

John writes, "I have no greater joy than to hear that my children are walking in the truth" (3 John 1:4), and then he describes that walk this way: "Beloved, it is a faithful thing you do in all your efforts for these brothers, strangers as they are." All your efforts. Multiple things are being done, and it doesn't matter to the doers if the efforts are for family or strangers. These people who John calls beloved are all-purpose Christians!

Then comes the contrast. Diotrephes was self-rising. John says, "I have written something to the church, but Diotrephes, who likes to put himself first, does not acknowledge our authority." Do you see how this fits in a study of happiness? "No greater joy" describes the all-purpose sisters and brothers, but the self-inflated Diotrephes is "not content" (3 John 1:9–10).

Another contrast comes in Mark 12. Jesus talks about "the scribes, who like to walk around in long robes and like greetings in the marketplaces and have the best seats in the synagogues and the places of honor at feasts" (vv. 38–39). How interesting that the very next thing that happens is that Jesus observes a woman giving all she has—two coins—and has this to say about her: "Truly, I say to you, this poor widow has put in more than all those who are contributing to the offering box. For they all contributed out of their abundance, but she out of her poverty has put in everything she had, all she had to live on" (vv. 43–44). We can be all about the show and the best seats, or we can put our whole life, "all we have to live on," into the cause of Christ. We can be all-purpose.

Who do you think was happier here? Jesus, Lord and Savior, commended the woman, but concerning the scribe, he said that he would receive the greater condemnation (Mark 12:40). If Mama ain't happy, she better check the label on the flour bag.

Look-at-Me Syndrome vs. Servitude: Haman vs. Mordecai

One of the most obvious contrasts between the self-rising and all-purpose individuals, and the ensuing happiness or lack thereof, is found in the book of Esther.

In the self-rising bag, you have this guy who has the worst case of look-at-me syndrome I have ever seen. After being promoted by the Persian king to a top post, Haman thrived on the bowing and kowtowing he received. If it takes a king's edict to cause people to act like they like you, it's a pretty empty victory. Nonetheless, it worked for Haman. In fact, in-between meltdowns of fury, Esther 5:9 says, "And Haman went out that day, joyful and glad of heart." Hold that thought, and that emotion.

In the all-purpose bag, you have Mordecai. The closer you look at the account, the more you appreciate Mordecai's all-purpose servitude. First of all, there was an orphaned cousin who needed a parent to step in and take over (Esther 2:7). Mordecai was all-purpose. When Esther was brought to the palace in a collection of beautiful women to be displayed to the king, someone needed to stay close by that gate to make sure all was well in Esther's new world (vv. 11, 21). Mordecai was all-purpose. There was a plot to kill the king, and someone needed to report it to save a life (v. 22). Mordecai was all-purpose. There was a law to worship a man as if he were God, and when everyone else was falling down at Haman's feet out of fear, someone needed to take a stand (Esther 3:2). Mordecai was all-purpose. When an entire nation was about to be wiped out in violent destruction, somebody had to do something (4:8). Mordecai was all-purpose. When his own adopted daughter was too fearful to stand up to the king, somebody had to set her straight (4:13). Mordecai was all-purpose.

But in the middle of these events, in contrast to the "joyful and glad of heart" description we mentioned of Haman, "Mordecai tore his clothes and put on sackcloth and ashes, and went out into the midst of the city, and he cried out with a loud and bitter cry" (Est. 4:1). That's because he was all-purpose. And as all-purpose Christians, when we respond to every need the best we can through the strength of God, sometimes that need is to cry, and we do it heart and soul.

Someone needed to take a stand.

Our discussion of these men can't end here. Haman's joy turned to heartburn like a habanero on the way down the digestive tract. Listen to how happy he really was:

> And Haman recounted to them the splendor of his riches, the number of his sons, all the promotions with which the king had honored him, and how he had advanced him above the officials and the servants of the king. [Talk about Bragfest 480 BC! I envision a cat yawning big in the corner, and everyone else wishing they could too.] Then Haman said, "Even Queen Esther let no one but me come with the king to the feast she prepared. And tomorrow also I am invited by her together with the king. Yet all this is worth nothing to me, so long as I see Mordecai the Jew sitting at the king's gate" (Est. 5:11–13).

His joy was so shallow and fragile that it was squelched by the thought that one person was living out there somewhere who refused to see him as the god who had arrived. By chapter 6, Haman is barreling to his house, ashamed, mourning with his head covered (Est. 6:12). By chapter 7, he's dead as a doornail, and by the first verse of chapter 8, everything he had owned belongs to Esther. Self-rising happiness gets moldy in a hurry.

But what happened to Mordecai? The last verse of the book reads,

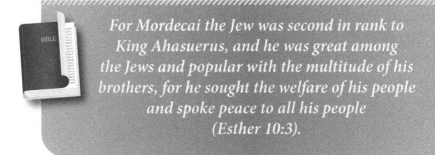

For Mordecai the Jew was second in rank to King Ahasuerus, and he was great among the Jews and popular with the multitude of his brothers, for he sought the welfare of his people and spoke peace to all his people (Esther 10:3).

What was his greatness? He sought the welfare of others. He spoke peace to people. He was all-purpose.

All-Purpose Women

Is Mama all-purpose? From every corner and food truck, someone is yelling about women being empowered. It usually means make more money, command more respect, and often even let go of old-school traditions of morality (which may be biblical in their basis). It smells like the self-rising flour bin. Rarely do we see genuine empowerment like Mordecai's: seek the welfare of others, speak peace to the people. But when we do, it comes straight out of the all-purpose bin, and it comes out laughing with a spring in its step.

When I was a student at a Christian university, Mrs. Delores was the president's wife. I'm sure she sat at the head table at many fancy dinners. Isn't that what a first lady does? That's the definition I have in my head.

I'm sure she did that, but it's not what I remember at all. I remember her having all the freshmen come over to her yard for a cookout. She served the dogs and burgers. I remember her working hard in an apron stirring chili for a school event. I remember her with a mop in what was then the banquet hall. One day, I was in the lobby of the auditorium, and I don't know why, but she was in there just sweeping away. I think it was because she saw something on the floor that needed sweeping up.

I know I'm Colombo and Monk rolled up into one here, but—it makes sense! It makes sense because she was all-purpose. And that day, as soon as I walked in the door, she started talking about a funny memory we shared, and pretty soon we were both laughing as she brought up similar memories involving others. What she was trying to do was encourage me as a student—as a young Christian woman. She was empowering me to have a happy life, in service. Or was she just sweeping the floor when I happened by?

God's providence allows all-purpose women to empower others just through doing what needs to be done at the time. And the ripple effect that comes from the joy of walking with God wherever the path leads and the plot twists are long-winding.

I'll be honest with you. It's been a hard week. I lost Joyce this week, my friend in Christ for sixteen years. She went suddenly, but about a year ago, we thought we were losing her then. At that point, everything that could be done had been done to fight her cancer. She lay and weakly but bravely discussed how she wanted to die, and where she wanted to die, not because of her own wishes, but because of what would be the least painful for others. We begged God.

I have come off my bed of affliction!

And then it happened. We got a phone call from Joyce, but it wasn't her weak, subdued voice. It was her chipper, enthusiastic greeting! And she said, "God has answered our prayers. I have come off of my bed of affliction, and I will be at church tomorrow!" She was true to her word. Not only that, but there was a little sign-up list on the board to buy puzzles and Bible storybooks for some special needs adults who had been quarantined in the pandemic of 2020. Joyce was the first one to grab a pen and start signing.

"Joyce!" I practically scolded her when she signed up to shop for a puzzle. She looked at me, picked up the pen again, and signed the other line to buy a storybook. "Wait, are you doing both?" I asked. Her answer was golden: "Why wouldn't I?"

Why Wouldn't I?

Why wouldn't I? It's the theme song for the all-purpose Christian. I would have to write another book to tell you all the ways that Joyce has been all-purpose, but suffice it to say, she lines up right behind Jesus, and just in front of Mordecai. But that's not the only awards ceremony she's nominated for. Few people have ever laughed as well, as hard, or as long. Ever: BC, AD or in a time warp. Her trials also have surpassed most people I have known or heard of, which further attests to the joy that comes from serving no matter your background or hardships.

The pretty college girls got prettier.

All-purpose can encompass some of the strangest things we could imagine. I put out a post a few years ago that I needed some Pringles cans for a teacher who was doing a Bible craft with children. These children would be at a huge brotherhood event, and people would drive long distances to arrive. I think we ended up with the world's largest Pringle can collection, not because one single person had any on hand to begin with, but because a whole lot of women were all-purpose. I know because their children told me: children from Texas, children from Colorado, children from Mississippi, children from everywhere! I kept hearing the same story: "Guess what? My mom went to the store and bought a bunch of potato chips, and we ate them all the way here. We usually eat grapes and carrots, but not today!"

A few years ago, I was at a ladies' event in Texas. I remember there being a row full of college girls there, and they were just strikingly beautiful. They were dressed up to the nines and had hair that was a ten. They were pretty much the picture of what each of us would trade an heirloom diamond to look like.

The building had water problems that morning. At first, there was no water, and then when I was speaking, there was a lot of hammering and prying going on. When the water did come back on, it really came on, and gushed out of the toilets in the bathroom.

That's when the pretty college girls got prettier. Here they came with big smiles on their faces, and a roll of paper towels in each hand. They got down on both knees and cleaned what needed to be cleaned. They were all-purpose with a capital A. And it seemed to be the driving force for their laughter and smiles.

Contrast this to the attitude of rising stars, political figures, and talented athletes. Mohammad Ali is attributed with the phrase, "It's hard to be humble, when you're as great as I am." James Brown said, "I've outdone anyone you can name—Mozart, Beethoven, Bach, Strauss." And Justin Bieber told *Billboard*, "I think, If I'm not on top, it would be because I didn't want to be." These quotes are not what other people said about these celebrities. They said this about themselves. And if you'll notice, the self-rising bag rarely sits next to the fun-size candy bars in the pantry. There's no fun in self-absorption.

If Mama Ain't Happy … You Know What

The church carries out her mission because Christians are all-purpose. Acts 4 Christians sold whatever they could of their own belongings because there was a need. Christians repeatedly take a week of vacation to become Bible camp counselors because there is a need. Church building roofs are repaired, campaign workers are fed, Bible bowl buzzers are connected, all because there is a deeper need to teach, evangelize, and care for the lost and hurting. And as a result, joy resounds from our buildings, our homes, and our very souls.

> "What do you want me to do for you?"
> ~Jesus

And James and John, the sons of Zebedee, came up to him and said to him, "Teacher, we want you to do for us whatever we ask of you." And he said to them, "What do you want me to do for you?" And they said to him, "Grant us to sit, one at your right hand and one at your left, in your glory" (Mark 10:35–37).

Wow. Has there ever been a clearer case of attempted self-promotion? They even got their mother involved if you read Matthew's account (Matt. 20:20).

And yet, it's incredible to realize that this same John, all about being front and center—well, slightly to the right—could, some time later, allow some of the most beautiful instruction from the Holy Spirit to flow out of his heart and pen to be treasured by generations on end. Some of my favorites:

> "My little children, I am writing these things to you so that you may not sin. But if anyone does sin, we have an advocate with the Father, Jesus Christ the righteous" (1 John 2:1).

> "Little children, let us not love in word or talk but in deed and in truth" (1 John 3:18).

> "Little children, you are from God and have overcome them, for he who is in you is greater than he who is in the world" (1 John 4:4).

John's brother James had died as a martyr for Christ's cause by this point (Acts 12:2). John, in a spirit of humility, was penning beautiful encouragement to love and stay the course. What took these two from self-rising to all-purpose? They had seen the Savior. They had watched as he was spat on, as spikes were driven through his palms, as he hung on a cross for hours on end unable to get a good breath . . . because he wanted to take the punishment for John's sins, for James's sins, for my sin. They had seen the bitter end, and then learned that it was the blessed beginning. They walked with the resurrected Savior and had a stark and perceptive realization of what happiness really is.

They walked with the resurrected Savior. May we all do the same.

And he said to them, "If anyone would be first, he must be last of all and servant of all"
(Mark 9:35).

 # If You're Happy, You Will Know It

1. Think of the most all-purpose Christian woman you've known. Of all the deeds you remember, which one stood out the most to you? Share that if you're in a group study.

2. Of the illustrations given of all-purpose Christians in this chapter, they range in age from very young to sages. Why is it particularly encouraging to see a young person getting joy from serving? And what is significant about an older person being all-purpose?

3. Find a verse in the book of Esther that communicates the essence of godly attitude. This week, write it down, underlining or circling important thoughts. Next, commit it to memory. Third, text it or mail it to one of your children or someone you work closely with telling them how it reminds you of them.

4. Among Christians, do you agree that people who work harder laugh harder? Why do you think this is true or not true?

5. Plan a visit this week with someone outside your age bracket, whether younger or older. Ideas: (1) Meet for a dessert or coffee; (2) Just show up at her home; (3) Plan to go visit a third homebound person together; (4) Cook something up in the kitchen together to share with a kids' class (or an adult class).

6. The book of Acts is full of examples of all-purpose Christians. One of those examples is mentioned. Find another all-purpose Christian in Acts. What did she/he do, and how is it meaningful to you personally?

Happy Trails

And speaking of driving . . .

In honor of the special days in May and June, let's affirm that there are two kinds of people. I would like to honor them both, for both make a huge number of sacrifices, both make it possible for us to get through our day-to-day challenges, and both bring a great deal of joy into our lives. I am referring, of course, to the two groups of people who both operate motorized vehicles, but who are distinctly categorized as the fun drivers and the practical drivers.

Most dads fit into the fun drivers subset. This is demonstrated most often in vacant parking lots in one of the following behaviors. Fun drivers will cut the wheel to make a "U," tricking the passengers into thinking there is a determined direction in which to go. However, instead of straightening the wheel to finish the "U," the wheel remains in position so that the car is making a continuous "O." Over and over again. This continues until someone throws up, or the person on the passenger side slaps the driver.

The second behavior was recently demonstrated to me and involves an obstacle course of shopping carts in which the driver who, at first, appears to be casually leaving the premises after a shopping excursion suddenly and with no warning, says, "Hey, watch how many buggies I can weave through without hitting any!" He proceeds to do so with increasing acceleration. This sometimes results in a related behavior, known as buggy-tipping.

The last behavior involves ice and snow when everyone else has left the church parking lot except for the minister and the deacon over building, grounds, and fun activity in both. Use your imagination.

Mom drivers are usually the practical ones. They get you to your orthodontist and science fair on time, but are pretty useless when it comes to counting how many reflectors you can hit in a five-second time limit, or seeing how many turns it takes to knock the Arby's cup off the roof.

This is precisely why dads make better driving instructors for teenagers. Dads are used to steering off the shoulder to hit a mud puddle or turning on the wipers randomly for no reason at all. This is why dad instructors say things like, "You're doing good, son. Straighten it out a little. Try not to clip the cow next time," and moms only know one word: "*Stop!*" This is said as she tries to pull her shin up through the floorboard and back into the car.

Since we have designated that most of the fun drivers are the dads and most of the practical drivers are the mothers, let's acknowledge that each group has its strengths. I find, in general and without being disrespectful of either gender, men excel in backing. Women, on the other hand, are creative, making figure eights, four hundred and seventy twos, and Mona Lisas on the way out of the driveway.

However, because of their confidence in backing, some men occasionally embark on it too enthusiastically. After all, if the speed limit is fifty-five, why waste time on twenty in reverse? Let's illustrate this principle with the real-life example of the preacher backing the church van into the elder's car with fervor on a campaign. This came in handy later for a sermon illustration concerning zeal which is not according to knowledge.

Because the practical drivers see driving as a task, a chore, they like to take breaks from it. Because the fun drivers see driving as a recreational pursuit, they stay on task as if it were overtime in a championship game.

So while moms say, "Who'd like to stop for a smoothie?" dads are like, "What? And stop the vehicle? Turn off the engine? Shatter all dreams for making the trip in a record eight-hour-and-sixteen-minute time?" Dad is not easily distracted by garage sale signs or threats that six bladders may simultaneously explode. All the passengers' limbs are going numb like cats on valium from a lack of circulation, and yet he adheres to the road like Joshua 1:7: "Turn not from it to the right hand or to the left."

Some ask what determines the tendency toward fun or practical. Is it just an X-Y chromosome thing? No, it's agreed upon by the majority of the Board of Certified Driver Analysts that it is more attributed to early childhood experiences with shopping buggies, which explains a lot in our family. My husband recounts the time he was pushing off with the left foot while keeping the right one on for stability, then hopping both feet on and coasting down the cereal aisle at breakneck speed before coming to a sudden halt when he rammed into the seat of a stranger's dress after which said stranger turned around and slapped him cold. True story; she did. That one instance forever designated him as one of the fun drivers. I, meanwhile and unbeknownst to him some 130 miles away, was steering a grocery cart down the cereal aisle to, of all things, put cereal in it. And that designated me in the practical group.

But as the ancient proverb says, it is better to dwell on the corner of the rooftop with Toucan Sam, Count Chocula and the Trix rabbit than to be on an aisle with a contentious woman hit by a speeding shopping cart.

Originally printed in Christian Woman *magazine, May/June 2014.*

CPSIA information can be obtained
at www.ICGtesting.com
Printed in the USA
JSHW031947200222
22977JS00004B/4

9 781945 127243